# Special Needs

# Language and Literacy

## Assessment Handbook

### for primary and secondary schools

**Gill Backhouse
and Prue Ruback**

HODDER
EDUCATION
AN HACHETTE UK COMPANY

D1475997

Hachette UK's policy is to use papers that are natural, renewable and recyclable products and made from wood grown in sustainable forests. The logging and manufacturing processes are expected to conform to the environmental regulations of the country of origin.

Orders: please contact Bookpoint Ltd, 130 Milton Park, Abingdon, Oxon OX14 4SB. Telephone: (44) 01235 827827. Fax: (44) 01235 400454. Lines are open 9.00–5.00, Monday to Saturday, with a 24-hour message answering service. Visit our website at www.hoddereducation.co.uk

First published in 2011 by Hodder Education, part of Hachette UK, 338 Euston Road, London NW1 3BH

Impression number  5   4   3   2   1
Year               2015   2014   2013   2012   2011

Typeset in 12 pt Palatino Light by Phoenix Photosetting, Chatham, Kent ME4 4TZ
Printed in Great Britain by Hobbs the Printers Ltd, Totton, Hampshire SO40 3WX

A catalogue record for this title is available from the British Library

ISBN: 978 1 444 12202 2

# Contents

# The authors

## Gill Backhouse

Gill is a Chartered Psychologist and Honorary Research Associate in the Division of Psychology and Language Sciences at University College London. She taught the OCR courses for Specialist Teachers at UCL and ran an assessment clinic there for children with Specific Learning Difficulties (SpLD).

Gill was an External Verifier and then Chief Verifier for the OCR SpLD courses. She worked in close collaboration with the JCQ Special Requirements Committee for several years, helping to develop the system for both Specialist Teachers and Educational Psychologists to report on students' needs for access arrangements during public examinations. She wrote the original Patoss/JCQ Guide on this subject, now in its fourth edition, and co-edited *Dyslexia? Assessing and Reporting: The Patoss Guide,** also published by Hodder Education.

## Prue Ruback

Prue is a Visiting Lecturer at the University of Hertfordshire; Lead Moderator for OCNLR Access Courses to HE; and training consultant for the London Borough of Brent. Formerly, she was Senior Lecturer in Primary Education at the University of Hertfordshire, working with trainee teachers, Teaching Assistants and postgraduates. Prue was course tutor for the OCR SpLD Courses at Harrow College for a number of years; also an External Verifier and then Chief Verifier for the scheme. She was a founder member of Patoss and was the Patoss Bulletin Editor for ten years. She trained as a primary school teacher, with particular interest in Early Years, Special Educational Needs and the teaching of reading. She still finds time to read avidly to her four small grandchildren!

## Hannah Williams *(Chapter 8)*

Hannah taught in East London for ten years, including five as a SENCO in Newham. She is now a member of the SpLD Team in Newham's Learning Support Service. Previously a Newham Tutor on the Graduate Certificate course in SpLD, she now delivers, with a colleague, the Post-Graduate Diploma in Special and Inclusive Education (SpLD-Dyslexia) in Newham, in conjunction with the Institute of Education, London.

---

* **Patoss** Professional Association of Teachers of Students with Specific Learning Difficulties

# Introduction

This book is about educational testing, for the most part working with pupils whose progress has given rise to some concern. Its aim is to enable SENCOs to develop professional standards when assessing children's language and literacy skills. The contents will equip staff with the basic tools needed to use tests and interpret the results with confidence, and to make recommendations for learning support and appropriate referrals where necessary.

The emphasis is on *what* to do and *how* to do it, in an accessible way with minimal theory. Specific tests which are moderately priced and available to the non-specialist are described, as well as informal methods of assessment. How to make the link between test results and IEP targets is discussed. Key principles of successful remedial techniques employed by dyslexia specialists are outlined.

The first chapter is a general one, covering the theory and practice of choosing and using tests.

The next six are of most relevance to primary school SENCOs, although many secondary staff who have to support pupils with very low literacy levels will find they contain much useful information.

The last two chapters are mainly of relevance to secondary school SENCOs. Chapter 8 offers advice regarding management issues as well as support for individual pupils. Chapter 9 focuses particularly on the issues surrounding access arrangements in the GCSE examinations, but also for National Tests.

The book also contains proforma letters, photocopiable resources such as informal tests and questionnaires, and checklists,* to support the busy SENCO in initial assessment and monitoring progress. Contact details of test publishers, relevant organisations, useful resources and further reading are provided at the end of the book.

For the sake of brevity, we have followed the convention of referring to all teachers as female and all pupils as male.

We would like to thank the following people: Hannah Williams and her colleagues in the London Borough of Newham's Learning Support Service for Chapter 8; Charles Knight of Hodder Education for his editorial support and encouragement; Jane Speake and Louise Green for their advice with regard to Chapters 2 and 9. The authors nevertheless take responsibility for any errors or omissions.

*Gill Backhouse and Prue Ruback*

---

* Also available as free web resources: visit this book's 'title' page on www.hoddereducation.co.uk.

# 1 Assessment: Theory and Practice

Learning difficulties develop over time. As soon as a class teacher begins to worry that a child is not making the same progress as his peers, the inevitable question is *Why?*

- Has he got a learning difficulty?
- Is he not able to concentrate and always out of his seat?
- Has he been away a lot?
- Does he get any support at home?

The causes may be **within child** – aspects of his own mental abilities which make it hard for him to learn certain skills at the same rate as his peers; or **environmental** – lack of appropriate teaching at crucial stages due to absence from school, poor teaching, emotional problems, or a combination of factors. Did he *miss the boat?*

Before trying to teach him the same things again, in the same way, an initial assessment should help to answer the *Why?* question and, more importantly, enable learning support (LS) to be planned which will begin to target the problem area in a more focused and effective way.

- Is there really a problem?

Experienced teachers, using the knowledge developed over many years and in different settings, will generally be confident in their judgement as to when a pupil is having problems. However, for less experienced teachers, who have perhaps only taught in one area (say a small rural village, or an inner-city school with large numbers of students whose first language is not English), knowing what is normal/average *nationally* at certain ages is not so easy. Furthermore, a personal assurance that there is no need to worry – '*He's just a late developer*' – may not be enough to satisfy worried parents and, indeed, may be wrong! Assessment before planning action is in *everyone's* best interests – pupil, staff and parents.

# What you need to know

## Formal assessment: standardised tests

The use of standardised tests will reveal, against *national* standards, how pupils are performing on certain skills compared with other pupils of similar age, regardless of where they live and what type of school they attend. In working out the average score on (say) a single-word reading test for 7 year olds or 14 year olds, the test developers will have included the results of hundreds of same-age pupils at all types of school across the country and come to a reliable conclusion. All the different factors which might affect pupils' reading and spelling skills – teaching methods, exposure to print, vocabulary, first language and so on – are taken into account due to the size of the sample. The resulting graphs for each age group (after some statistical procedures) are the familiar bell-shaped curves and referred to as **normal distributions**. Test development is an extremely labour-intensive and thus costly business, due to the mass testing required across the age ranges in order to produce scores which are reliable. This is the reason why tests are often expensive to buy.

Tests standardised on rather few pupils, and perhaps in just one area of the country and/or decades ago, are less likely to represent the current picture across the population as a whole. So, the golden rule is:

> **Only use tests developed in recent years by a reputable publisher, who has the resources to do the development and standardisation properly.**

A second imperative is:

> **Only use tests where the chronological age of the pupil(s) you are assessing is comfortably within the lower and upper age limits of the test.**

For technical reasons, test results are less likely to be valid if the age of the pupils with whom you are working is very close to the upper, or lower, limits of the age range of the test.

Standardised tests are basically used in two ways:

- for screening purposes
- in individual assessment.

In both cases you need to understand how to administer tests and interpret the results in a professional way.

**Screening** involves the use of the same test for a whole class of pupils to identify those falling below a certain standard. *Where* to set the benchmark – the bottom 1% or 5%, say – is a decision which will be determined by the SENCO. Children falling below this benchmark will then benefit from further individual assessment and follow-up.

**Individual Assessment** involves the use of one or more tests to investigate an individual pupil's strengths and weaknesses. This will enable careful observation of how he tackles each task – easily, or slowly and with much effort – and noting the nature of his errors.

# What is a standardised test?

The essential features are:

1   **The materials used (the test items) are the same for everyone**. No photocopied materials from who knows where: only the original publisher's materials.

2   **The administration, including the exact words used to ask the questions, and perhaps the time allowed for response, is the same for everyone.** The test manual will tell you precisely how to administer the test and whether, for example, you may repeat a question. You must not phrase questions differently if the pupil has not understood the first time round, but (if allowed) you might simply repeat it.

> **By altering any aspect of the test materials or administration you are likely to invalidate the results.**

During the assessment session, a quiet, well-lit room, a reassuring explanation of the purpose of the test and the nature of ongoing feedback, are also important variables. Resist the urge to praise a correct response, because when you then do not say *'Well done'* or *'Good'* after the next response, the pupil will immediately suspect he has got that one wrong and may get upset or flustered. Aim for an encouraging but non-committal *'Thank you'* or a smile and a nod quickly followed by *'And the next one is...'*. Make sure you know where to start, given the pupil's chronological age/year group. Some tests will give rules for backtracking to easier items if the pupil fails on some of the first items administered.

3   **The scoring method is the same for everyone.** Most test manuals will give very precise instructions as to what may be counted as correct. Make sure you read the instructions carefully, and follow them to the letter.

If you adhere to these principles, all pupils will have, as far as possible, the same experience and so differences in standardised scores should reflect true differences in the knowledge or skill being tested.

# Interpreting test scores

### Raw scores

In the first instance, what you will have is the **raw score** – the total number of correct responses. Some tests have slightly different ways of working out the raw score (e.g. instead of simply counting up the number of correct responses, you might need to work out the total number of responses *minus* the number which were incorrect). Make sure you have ascertained the proper method for the test you are using. Some tests allow skipping of early items which are well within the competence of a particular pupil, in which case be careful to add the marks for these skipped items to the final raw score.

## Standardised scores: mean and standard deviation

During the test development, an exactly average score for each age group is worked out – i.e. the sum of all the raw scores divided by the number of pupils of that age who completed the test. This is called the **mean**.

However, a *range* around the exact average is obviously needed to encompass results which are very close to the mean and to avoid labelling large numbers of scores as *above* or *below average*. There is a standard method of working out where the boundaries between the average *range* and those scores above and below it, lie for each test. The distance between the *mean* and these boundaries is called the **standard deviation** (SD).

All the data from the original trials of the test are converted onto a **standard scale**, the distance from bottom to top measuring exactly six standard deviations (see Figure 1.1).

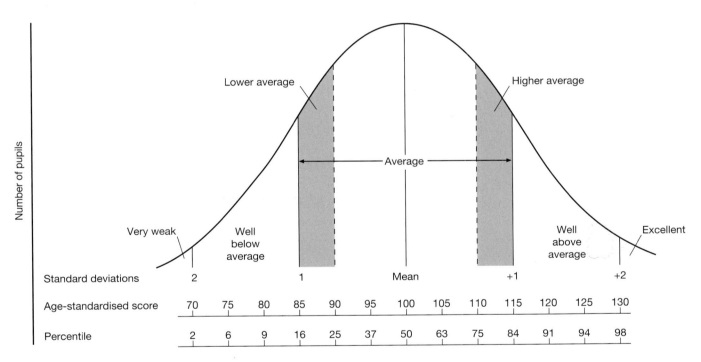

**Figure 1.1:** The normal distribution curve

The scale most often used for educational tests has a mean of 100 and SD of 15. Any raw score can now be converted into a **standardised score** (SS), and will fall within three standard deviations either side of the mean, using the appropriate **norm tables** (i.e. for the age of the pupil you are assessing).

It is a statistical fact that the group falling within one standard deviation either side of the mean includes the middle 66% of pupils. So if the mean on a test is 100 and the SD is 15, scores between 85 and 115 would fall within the 'average' two-thirds band. Similarly, if the mean is 50 and the SD is 10 (e.g. *Cognitive Abilities Test* scores), results between 40 and 60 would fall within this 'average' band.

It is sometimes useful to refer to individuals whose scores are nearly but not quite outside the middle band as having *low* or *high* average scores (see Figure 1.1).

## Percentiles

Most test manuals offer **percentile scores** – as well as standardised scores – but these are easily misinterpreted.

A percentile score shows the percentage of same-age pupils who score at or below the one you are considering. So a test result at the 50th percentile is exactly average; a score at the 10th percentile is quite low (as 90% of pupils would have higher scores); and a score at the 80th percentile is rather good, as 80% of pupils would obtain lower scores. Note that these percentages relate to the *national* population, and are not necessarily reflected in your own class or school.

However, there is a very common misconception about percentile scores *slightly* above or below the mean. This stems from the shape of the normal curve. For example, some might mistakenly think that a pupil with a spelling test standardised score of 105 is a *much* better speller than another who scores 95, since the equivalent percentile scores are about 37 and 63. But look at the graph (Figure 1.1) and you can see that there are almost as many pupils (left-hand vertical axis) with scores at 95 as at 100 or 105 (bottom horizontal axis).

> **So, do not over-interpret small differences between standardised scores which are close to the mean.**

However, a difference of 10 scale points between two standardised scores which are *further away* from the mean (say between 70 and 80, or 115 and 125, on the bottom axis) represents a large difference in performance compared to the average. Comparatively few pupils have very high or low scores which fall at the extremes of the normal (bell-shaped) curve.

## Test ages or age equivalents

Reading and Spelling 'Ages' are often quoted and show the chronological age at which a particular raw score is the *average* for the pupils in the standardisation group – so if the average raw score for all pupils aged 8 years 6 months on a given reading test is 25, *any* pupil scoring 25 on the same test may be said to have a reading age of 8 years 6 months (usually shown as 8:6, but sometimes as 8.5 years). Like percentiles, test ages can be very misleading in certain circumstances – especially when used for older pupils.

Children are developing all sorts of skills and abilities very much faster when in the primary school than later on, and on measures such as shoe sizes, word recognition, or spelling, say, the average for pupils aged from 6 to 6:6 will be significantly less than the average for pupils a year older. However, the differences between 15 and 16 year olds will be much less; and between

40 and 50 year olds, next to nothing. Therefore, many tests give averages for quite small age bands for younger pupils (typically for each 2 to 3 months of age) and then gradually expand the age bands for secondary students (from 6 months to a year by late adolescence) and adults (to as much as 10-year age bands).

This is an important point to bear in mind if using **age equivalents/test ages** when discussing results. Whilst it is fairly meaningful, and useful when choosing reading material, to say that an 8 year old has a *reading age* (RA) of 6, it would be most dispiriting to tell a 15 year old he had an RA of 10 – when in fact he might only have failed to read a few less words on the test than needed to gain an average score for his age.

So, another golden rule is:

> ## *NEVER* use 'age' scores beyond Key Stage 2.

One last point about differences between scores – say between Pupil A and Pupil B – or Pupil A's scores when you *re*test to monitor progress: educational testing lacks the precision of physical measurement (of height, for example) and a pupil may achieve slightly different results on another occasion. This may be sheer luck – knowing how to spell a word just as difficult or unusual as another he did not know. Or his results may have been affected by a variety of factors such as fatigue, mood, his attitude towards the tester, and so on. Randomly ticking boxes on a comprehension test will produce *some* correct answers by chance!

Lengthier test manuals provide data regarding *standard errors of measurement*, *confidence intervals* and *probability coefficients* which enable you to allow for these factors in your conclusions. However, some training in statistics/ psychometrics is needed to interpret test results with this level of accuracy. The really important point is that, when monitoring progress, you should look for quite *big* differences between standardised scores (say 5 to 10 points) that a pupil obtains from one occasion to another, before you report *real* improvement.

In summary, always try to explain and use standardised scores when talking to colleagues or parents, to avoid misleading them about how far behind his peers a pupil is falling, or the amount of progress he has made following intervention. Test 'ages' do not provide a good basis on which to assess and report longer-term progress.

## Choosing a test

A key issue is to choose a test which actually measures what you need to know and which provides useful information for planning Learning Support (LS) – see Chapters 3, 4 and 6 for specific examples. Are you worried about reading accuracy, or trying to reassure parents that their son's reading comprehension is satisfactory? A single test is unlikely to do both.

- Look carefully at the test publishers' catalogues or websites and ask to see inspection copies of reading and spelling tests which might be suitable for your school.

- Look in the manual and find out when the test was developed and standardised. If the edition you are using is more than ten years old, try and find a test of more recent origin.

- Also check the spread of schools used to standardise the test – was there a good, wide representative sample?

- Check the age range of the test – you should not administer tests to pupils whose ages are at the extremes of, or outside, the age range of the test. Generally, in a learning support context where pupils' performance might be well below what is 'average' for their age, a 'wide-range' test is likely to be more helpful than a 'year-on-year' test.

- Is the test available in parallel forms? Many tests are standardised with parallel, or equivalent, forms (typically called Form A and Form B) which will give you comparable results without the pupil having to re-take the *same* test, This might be important if you want to re-test to assess the effectiveness of any special teaching or intervention.

- Beware of using the same form of any test repeatedly with the same pupil – the pupil's growing familiarity with the test will invalidate your results. Generally you should allow at least six months (with Key Stage 1 pupils) or a year (with older pupils) before re-using the same one.

- Make sure you are qualified to use the test(s) chosen. Some are 'closed' and their use is restricted to teachers with specialist training or other professionals. Most Hodder tests are freely available to schools, but both GL Assessment and Pearson Assessment publish tests whose use is restricted. You need to consult the catalogues regarding user eligibility.

- If there are some interesting-looking tests in the cupboard or filing cabinet at school (especially with lots of photocopied bits!), always check them against the criteria listed above before using them.

- Similarly, take a fresh look at any favourite test you have been using for many years.

## Ethics, confidentiality and data protection

When concerns are raised about a pupil's progress, it is important to prepare the ground with him and his parents/carers before embarking on any formal testing. Figure 1.2 provides a sample proforma letter, or you may prefer to develop your own.

Pupils need to know:

- why you are using tests;
- that the results will only be revealed to them, their parents and those teachers and other professionals involved in supporting them – on a need to know basis;

SCHOOL

LOGO

DATE

Dear . . . . . . . . . . . . . .

We have noticed that *[Name]* seems to be/is still finding it difficult to make progress with his reading/learning his spellings/producing written work/writing legibly *[i.e. define the concern]* and are keen to help him address the problem. This will involve some assessment which will be carried out by *[name & position]* on *[date]* in school.

To help understand his present difficulties, information about his general development is extremely useful and so I enclose a questionnaire, which I would ask you to complete and return to me by *[date]* either by hand or as an email attachment. *[NB make provision for parents with literacy difficulties – offer to do it by phone or face to face; parents whose first language is not English may need a translator.]*

Please be assured that **all** information provided will be treated with complete confidentiality and kept in a locked filing cabinet at all times, and only for as long as it is useful. Personal information will not be disclosed to anyone else without your express permission.

Would you be able to come and discuss the results with *[name of class teacher or tutor and/or teaching assistant]* and me on *[date/time]* so we can plan how to help *[Name]*? Please let me know by *[date]* if this is convenient or not.

With kindest regards,

Name

Position

Telephone

Email

**Figure 1.2:** Sample letter to parents/carers

■ that their results will be kept in a secure place;

■ that their data will only be kept for as long as needed.

This is not only good practice and common courtesy, but also essential under the law (Data Protection Act). Test users are also required to keep unused test manuals and record sheets secure, so that they are not available for anyone to use/misuse/photocopy/practise on and thus destroy their validity and usefulness. Remember how much work and expense went into developing them in the first place!

## Informal assessment

An alternative to using standardised tests is to find out more informally whether a pupil can demonstrate the particular skills or knowledge which are known to be important if progress is to be made – e.g. reading for meaning **and** decoding when reading; letter sound knowledge **and** segmentation skills in relation to spelling.

Research has shown unequivocally that phonological awareness is an important precursor to the acquisition and development of reading and spelling skills – and so, whether a pupil is five or ten years old, these skills need to be developed or secure. Using a standardised test such as the *Phonological Abilities Test* (PAT) or the *Phonological Assessment Battery* (PhAB) will tell you whether a pupil's skills in this regard are age-appropriate, or not – and of course enable you to target weaker areas.

But you could equally well, quickly and informally, test out whether or not a pupil can perceive and count syllables – and, if not, start training him in this important skill (see Chapter 3). This may well be a huge breakthrough for many older pupils who have never been taught how to tackle longer words.

Similarly, we know that both bottom-up (decoding) *and* top-down (reading for meaning) skills are important when reading (see the 'Simple Model of Reading', in Chapter 4). Using an informal technique such as **miscue analysis**, we can informally assess whether a child is *barking at print* (decoding without understanding), or reading very inaccurately but making an excellent attempt to grasp the meaning. This will not tell us how far behind the norm for his age he is, but will give information about his current strategies. This knowledge is vital if he is to be effectively helped to develop and improve his skills.

## Practical assessment

Before an individual assessment session with the pupil, you should:

■ inform the family and investigate his developmental history;

■ ensure vision and hearing checks have been recently carried out.

The sample letter in Figure 1.2 might be adapted for your own use, and the questionnaire in Figure 1.3 photocopied or adapted if necessary, using the web resource available at www.hoddereducation.co.uk.

In addition to gathering all this information, you also need to:

■ consult school records and all staff who know the pupil;

■ define the problem from everyone's point of view – pupil, parents and teaching staff;

■ consider which assessment techniques will be the most useful for finding out about his problems – informal methods and/or standardised tests.

## The assessment session – Dos and Don'ts

■ Make sure the pupil has not done the test before in school – or at least within the previous year.

■ Make sure nobody else has administered the same test recently; sometimes parents may have arranged a private assessment, which included the same tasks.

■ Try and use tests which have parallel forms, so that you can use Form A first and Form B next time. Otherwise, 'practice effects' may invalidate the results.

■ Make sure you know exactly how to administer the test (including the start and stop rules).

■ Collect all the equipment you will need – record sheets, pencils, stopwatch, clipboard, rewards, etc.

■ Ensure the pupil is comfortable – does not need the WC or some water.

■ Make sure that the room is well lit, quiet and you will not be interrupted.

■ Explain what is going to happen, why and how long it will take. For younger children, a star chart or certificate (e.g. see pages 18–19) is highly motivating – let him stick a star on for each test completed and then write a complimentary note underneath for him to take back to class.

■ When introducing each test, explain that there is no pass or fail, but that it is a means of finding out just what he can do and where his difficulties (if any) lie, so the problem can be tackled.

■ Explain that you will stop if/when the questions get too hard.

■ Arrange yourself with a clipboard so you can make notes and record responses without the pupil seeing what you are writing – especially ticks and crosses. It is usually best to sit at right angles to the pupil (on the right if you are right-handed and to the left if you are left-handed).

■ Explain the purpose of each test to the pupil – you might even ask if he would prefer to do the reading or writing first. Let him know regularly how much longer the session will be, and do not over-test.

# BACKGROUND QUESTIONNAIRE

*In order to understand any learning difficulties your child may have, information regarding his/her development is vital. Please complete this confidential questionnaire, giving as much relevant detail as possible.*

**Child's full name:**                          **Date of birth:**

## FAMILY BACKGROUND

Position in family – please give ages of any brothers and sisters

First language of family/language mainly spoken at home

Any history of language difficulties, or reading/spelling problems in the immediate or extended family?

## PHYSICAL DEVELOPMENT

Were the pregnancy and birth normal?

Were there any difficulties with feeding?

Was he/she early, average, or late to sit up, crawl and walk? *(give ages if possible)*

Did he/she learn to feed him/herself, get dressed, etc, quite easily?

Is he/she right- or left-handed?

Is he/she physically well co-ordinated or awkward?

Any serious illnesses or accidents?                          Any allergies? *(give details)*

Any chronic medical conditions?

Does he/she take any long-term medication? If so, please specify.

Has he/she suffered unduly from colds and ear infections? If so, at what age(s)?

Any problems with hearing?                          Date of last hearing test:

Any problems with vision (incl. squint)?                          Date of last eyesight test:

## LANGUAGE & SPEECH DEVELOPMENT

Was he/she early, average, late in learning to talk?

Is he/she a talkative child?

Does he/she have any difficulty in expressing him/herself?

Have there been any problems with pronunciation?     Yes/No
If so, please give details.

Has he/she ever seen a Speech & Language Therapist?   Yes/No
If so, please say *why, when* and for *how long*.

## TEMPERAMENT

How would you describe your child's personality?

Is he/she *(please underline the descriptions which are most appropriate)*:
- happy with own company            average       very sociable and outgoing?
- highly-strung and easily upset      average       very placid and easy-going?

Has he/she ever had any problems that seemed of emotional origin?
If so, please give details.

## INTERESTS

What kind of activities does your child seem to favour (if any)?
For example: social; practical; active; artistic; musical; computer games; TV; books.

Please list all regular activities that your child attends out of school (e.g. Cubs, swimming, language lessons).

## SCHOOL WORK

Are there any problems at home to do with homework, reading practice, etc?

Has he/she had any extra help with learning from a private tutor or a Kumon class?
If so, please give details.

Any other relevant information?

**Figure 1.3:** Questionnaire for parents/carers

- Tell the pupil that you need to look carefully at the results and think how it would be best to help him. When you have done this, a meeting will be arranged so that all concerned – the pupil, his parents, his class teacher or other staff – can discuss the issues and make plans to address them.

- Mark the test papers carefully according to the test protocols. Make sure you have worked out the pupil's exact age correctly (usually in years and *completed* months) and convert the raw scores to standardised scores using the correct table of norms.

- Make brief notes regarding his behaviour during the test session (anxious, confident, poor concentration, etc) and look at the nature of his errors (see Chapters 3 and 4).

- Summarise your findings in a format that you can easily refer to during subsequent meetings.

**Jack Smith**

*Jack worked really hard with me this morning and earned every one of these stars.*

*Well done Jack!*

*G. Backhouse*
*22/10/10*

**Figure 1.4a**

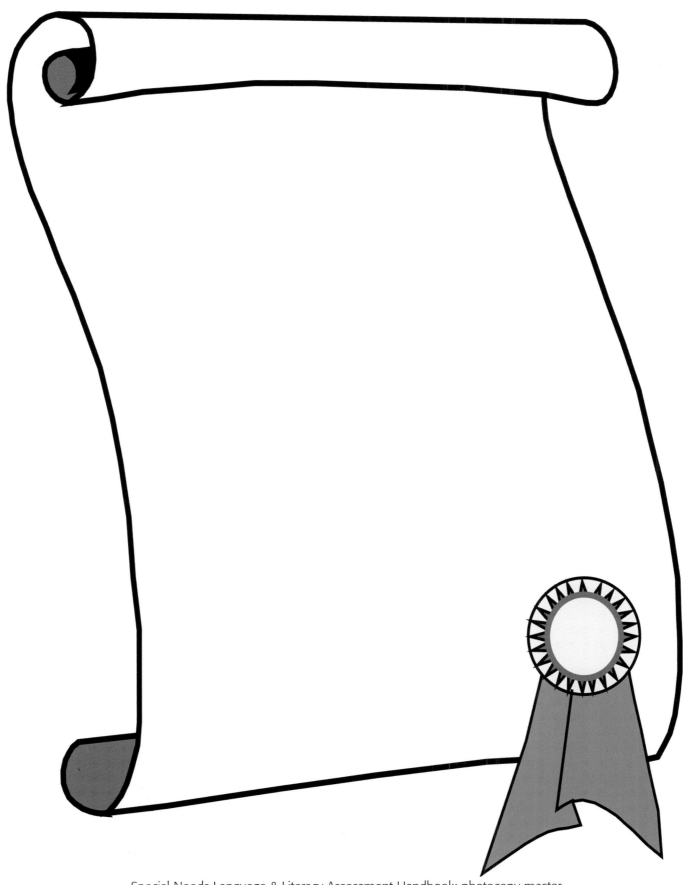

Special Needs Language & Literacy Assessment Handbook: photocopy master

**Figure 1.4b**

## Key points

Set up a meeting with the pupil (if appropriate), his parents, and relevant staff.

At the meeting:

- Explain your findings and discuss possible support strategies.
- Agree SMART targets for his IEP and a date for review.
  **S** – specific,
  **M** – measurable,
  **A** – attainable, achievable,
  **R** – relevant,
  **T** – time-based (e.g. *In 6 weeks time …, By the end of term …*)

If appropriate …

- Refer the pupil for further assessment by a Specialist Teacher (a teacher with a postgraduate qualification in the assessment and teaching of pupils with specific learning difficulties), Educational Psychologist (EP) or Speech and Language Therapist (SLT).

- Consider the pupil's need/eligibility for special **access arrangements** during National Tests or public examinations such as GCSE or Music exams (see Chapter 9).

# Speech, Language and Communication

# What you need to know

It is estimated that about 5% of children starting school may have speech and/or language difficulties, which impair their educational and/or social development. Subtle difficulties may exist which become serious barriers to learning as the demands on listening and speaking skills increase. Spoken language is the foundation on which literacy skills are based, and so a difficulty or delay in any aspect of language acquisition may have a knock-on effect on learning to read or write. We now know that *phonological awareness* (see Chapter 3) is a key issue in many children's problems with these basic skills.

Early identification of specific language problems is vital. Language problems may be misconstrued as general learning difficulties, causing much frustration in a child of normal intelligence. There is a particular danger of not noticing language problems in children with English as an Additional Language (EAL) and wrongly attributing difficulties to their bilingual status.

So, if a class teacher expresses concerns about a child's ability to understand when spoken to, and/or to express himself appropriately for his age, these should be taken seriously by the SENCO and investigated fully.

Language, as an academic discipline, is a complex subject with its own vocabulary and concepts. A brief introduction to some of these is now provided to aid access to further information, help you use assessment resources and support materials with understanding, and liaise with other professionals in an informed way.

## Aspects of language

Communication is a two-way process which involves both listening and speaking.

■ **Receptive language skills** refer to the process of listening and understanding language.

■ **Expressive language skills** refer to language output – speaking in a meaningful way that is appropriate in the social and cultural context.

Language skills can be further divided into **speech** (including prosody), **grammar**, **semantics** and **pragmatics**.

### Speech
Clear speech depends on both:

1  The *physical* ability to make the required sounds with the vocal apparatus – tongue, lips and vocal folds ('cords'): usually called **articulation**. Children with

cleft palate, severe dental problems or oral dyspraxia, for example, may not be able to produce the full range of sounds – even though they know which sounds they want to make.

2    The *mental/cognitive* knowledge of which sounds to make and in what order they are needed to convey a particular meaning (**phonology**). For example, the addition of one extra phoneme /**t**/ changes *rip* to *trip.* Then, by adding the phoneme /**s**/ in the initial or final position, the meaning of the word can change in two distinct ways: *strip* or *trips.*

Classic examples of phonological error include involuntary spoonerisms (e.g. *chish and fips, par cark*) and malapropisms (e.g. *fire distinguisher*). The speaker knows what he means but has retrieved a faulty sound sequence.

'Word finding' difficulties occur when a pupil cannot think which sequence of sounds is required to express a particular meaning and resorts to 'You know', 'The thingy' or gesture. Persistent difficulty in correctly ordering the sequence of phonemes in longer words (e.g. *hopsital*) is a common symptom of underlying phonological processing difficulties.

Children who display these tendencies far more frequently than their peers, or whose vocabulary development is clearly not progressing at an average rate, should be noted.

*Note:* When *speaking* (but not writing) in English we use 44 phonemes: 20 vowel sounds and 24 consonants. The number and type of vowels and consonants varies according to the language spoken. So children with EAL may appear to have articulation difficulties, which in reality stem from their own language pattern, rather than an impairment of any kind.

The **prosodic** aspects of speech – rhythm, syllable stress and intonation – are beginning to be recognised as key factors in the development of phonological awareness and thus to literacy acquisition.

## Grammar

Grammar can be defined at two levels:

1    **Syntax** (sentence structure). Problems with syntactic formation/sentence construction can often be seen in written work or noticed while a child is talking – for example 'Cat to old for catch a mouse' for '(My) cat (is) too old (to) catch a mouse'.

2    **Morphology** (word structure). This includes the ability to pluralise nouns and form the correct past tenses of verbs, both regular and irregular – for example house > houses, run > ran, talk > talked.

It is a normal stage of development in young children to show immature speech patterns when they are striving to form irregular past tenses, use pronouns or plurals – for example 'Mummy *telled* me to ….', 'The cat got two *mouses*', 'Where us going?' However, noticeably immature grammar (compared to his peers) would be a cause for concern.

## Semantics

Semantics refers to the *meaning* that underpins language. Semantic difficulties may affect both receptive and expressive language. Problems in expressive language will usually be very obvious, because the listener cannot understand what the child is trying to say. Receptive language difficulties may not always be noticed in the busy classroom context, but will inevitably affect reading comprehension.

## Pragmatics

This refers to the shared understanding of the context of words – the meaning that goes way beyond the literal. For example, as adults we know that an *'alarmed doors'* notice does not mean that the doors in a building are feeling nervous! Non-verbal cues – like facial expression, gesture and eye contact – add meaning to what we say and how we understand other people. Rules of conversation such as turn-taking – largely unspoken and unwritten – are nonetheless operating. Children who do not communicate appropriately find it difficult to interact with their peers and make friends. Severe and long-standing social communication difficulties are a feature of **autistic spectrum disorders** (ASD) (including Asperger's Syndrome), diagnosis of which may only be made by appropriately qualified professionals.

## Warning signs

At **Key Stage 1**, staff may note the following indicators:

- A child with particularly poor attention and listening skills.

- Obvious difficulties in understanding what he hears.

- He is confused by instructions and does not respond until he can see what other children are doing and then copies them.

- He asks the same questions, or asks for clarification, repeatedly.

- He does not always understand stories or explanations.

- He misunderstands questions and so does not respond appropriately.

- Language output is immature and the child's ability to express himself clearly is way below the standards of his peers.

- Social difficulties may be present. The child plays exclusively with younger children, or lacks friendships due to his poor communication skills.

By **Key Stage 2** there may, in addition, be particular difficulties with reading comprehension. Reading accuracy may be satisfactory – but the child fails to understand the point, gives inappropriate answers, cannot use inference and deduction, seems unable to make use of context clues.

Written language will be poor, with little structure, poor grammar and very limited vocabulary (often with over-use of common words like *good/nice*). Even when the pupil is offered the opportunity to dictate his work or ideas to someone else, the output is significantly below class expectations. By Year 6, poor literacy skills form a huge barrier to learning right across the curriculum.

Emotional and/or behaviour problems may now be significant, owing to frustration and loss of confidence.

# Practical assessment

Underpinning any formal assessment are good **observation** skills: time spent working with the child and seeing how he uses his speech and language skills, in the classroom and the playground, will be time well spent and will enrich any subsequent testing. Where concerns are raised, the following resources will be helpful.

### The Afasic Checklists
(Speake, J., 2003, LDA)

These resources provide an informal but sound method of gathering information about a child's speech and language skills over time. The questionnaires should be gradually completed by staff in close contact with the child over several weeks, so that responses are based on careful observation and are thus reliable.

The 4–5 years checklist enables the Early Years practitioner to observe communication skills which the child has secured. The 6–10 questionnaire focuses on potential problems. A simple scoring system and benchmarks for totals provide a basis for knowing when it is appropriate to a refer a pupil to speech and language therapy services as well as planning in-school learning support (LS).

The checklists are published in Speake, J. (2003) *How to identify and support children with speech and language difficulties*, published by LDA. This highly accessible book also contains much valuable information regarding support strategies which can be easily implemented by staff in the mainstream primary school.

### British Picture Vocabulary Scale (BPVS3)
(Dunn, L. M. et al, 2010, GL Assessment)

Additional information can be gained from administering the **BPVS**. Now in its third edition, this well known and widely used test is quick to administer (about 10 minutes).

Whilst a student's vocabulary is only a part of the whole picture with regard to his language competence, it is a fundamental issue and a convenient starting point when problems are suspected.

The **BPVS3** can be used with pupils from 3 to 15 years. Of particular use in many primary schools are the norms for children with EAL, at three stages – Early Years Foundation Stage (EYFS), Year 1 and Year 3.

It does not require the pupil to speak at all and so the BPVS is specifically targeting **receptive** vocabulary – how many words does the pupil understand when he hears them?*

Each test item consists of four coloured pictures of common items or actions. The teacher says the name of just one and the pupil must choose which picture to point to.

Establishing a 'basal' (where to start) and 'ceiling' (where to stop) can be a little tricky and so you must make sure you read and understand the rules for administration and scoring before using this test for real.

A standardised score in the below-average range (see Chapter 1) would indicate that a pupil is unlikely to understand some of the language output he hears each day. The **Age Equivalent** score will help Key Stage 1 and Key Stage 2 staff to be aware of the language level at which the child is comfortable (but please note the warnings in Chapter 1 about using test 'age' scores in the secondary phase).

*Note:* In order to purchase and use this *standardised* test (see Chapter 1) you must register as a test user with the publisher, GL Assessment.

# The case history

Information about the development of a child's speech and language skills is essential for understanding any present difficulties. In the first instance this will be obtained from his parents/carers, who must be informed about any concerns and involved from the start of an investigation. School records such as EYFS profile and transfer records between phases should also be consulted and may be a source of useful developmental information.

Figures 2.1 and 2.2 provide photocopiable questionnaires which can be used as a basis for finding out about the speech and language background. Information may also be available from EYFS settings. The questions cover a variety of *warning signs* and include *at risk* factors. Detail entered in the **Comments** column will be particularly useful when considering the likely causes of a pupil's difficulties. Do *within child* factors seem to be involved, or are there clear *environmental* factors at play?

For bilingual children, it will be important to probe the background in a sensitive way. Ideally you would have the assistance of someone who is a native speaker of the child's home language.

---

* Vocabulary tests where the pupil has to explain what words mean, require the use of **expressive** language skills in order to respond and are thus more demanding and likely to generate different results (e.g. the *Mill Hill Vocabulary Scale*, which is included with the *Ravens Matrices Tests*).

# SPEECH AND LANGUAGE
## questionnaire for English-speaking pupils

**Pupil's name:**                           **Date of birth:**

**Information acquired by:**             **Date:**

| Risk factors | Notes/comments |
|---|---|
| Any history of language and/or literacy difficulties in the family (parents, grandparents, siblings, aunts, uncles, cousins)? | |
| Complications during the pregnancy or birth? | |
| Prematurity? | |
| Postnatal health of child | |
| Late learning to speak (even slightly delayed, e.g. compared to siblings)? | |
| Recurring ear infections/ glue ear/grommets? | |
| Referred to SLT by Health Visitor following routine developmental check? | |
| Delay in mastering correct pronunciation of certain sounds (e.g./y/)? | |

| | |
|---|---|
| Had a brief course of SLT and then judged as no longer in need of support? | |
| Still difficult to understand at age 3 because of poor pronunciation and/or grammar? | |
| History of stammering? Resolved or ongoing? | |
| Problems with self-expression?<br>■ difficulty learning new words<br>■ mispronounces long words<br>■ overuses gesture<br>■ uses 'empty' vocabulary (e.g. 'thingy', 'you know')<br>■ becomes frustrated when speaking. | |
| Has problems:<br>■ remembering what has been told?<br>■ following instructions? | |
| Copies other children? | |
| Has difficulty understanding stories/texts? Does not respond appropriately to questions? | |
| Has difficulty making friends? Plays with younger children? | |

*Note:* If English is an additional language for a child's *family*, this may affect the child's language development in English.

Special Needs Language & Literacy Assessment Handbook: photocopy master

**Figure 2.1:** Speech and Language questionnaire – background information for English-speaking pupils, from birth to present

# SPEECH AND LANGUAGE

## questionnaire for EAL pupils

**Pupil's name:**                                   **Date of birth:**

**Information acquired by:**                     **Date:**

|  | Notes/comments |
|---|---|
| What language is used at home?<br>■ by parents, grandparents, siblings, child?<br>■ when watching TV?<br>■ when attending social/religious gatherings?<br>■ when playing with friends? |  |
| Was child speaking quite well by the time he/she was 2–3 years old?<br><br>Is he/she now completely fluent in his/her mother tongue? |  |
| Is pupil attending classes outside school to learn to read and write in this language? |  |
| How long has pupil been attending school in the UK? |  |
| If he/she has been to school in another country:<br>■ What language was used?<br>■ For how long did he/she attend? |  |
| In UK, has EAL support been provided, and for how long? |  |

Special Needs Language & Literacy Assessment Handbook: photocopy master

**Figure 2.2:** Speech and Language questionnaire – background information for pupils with EAL

> **Key points**
>
> With checklists or test results, together with case history information, you are now in a position to make an informed decision as to whether an immediate referral to a speech and language therapist and/or an educational psychologist is warranted, but also to institute some initial learning support appropriate to the child's needs. The completed questionnaires will provide extremely useful additional information for other professionals, from a diagnostic point of view.

# Learning support

The following resources are recommended:

- Single A4 size *Handy Hints* sheets on **Language Development** from the **Afasic** website: www.afasic.org.uk

- You can also download a number of *Glossary* sheets from the same source on a variety of language difficulties (e.g. developmental language delay/disorder; selective mutism; Asperger's syndrome; stammering)

- A series of highly accessible booklets, DVDs and posters on language development and how to promote essential communication skills are available from www.ican.org.uk (go to the **Talking Point** section)

- Speake, J. (2003) *How to Identify and Support Children with Speech and Language Difficulties.* LDA

- Baldwin, L. (2008) *Receptive Language Difficulties. Practical strategies to help children understand spoken language.* LDA

**Referral** to Speech & Language Therapy Services/Advisory Teacher for Speech & Language.

Make sure you are familiar with the correct referral procedures in your authority.

**Professional organisations** (for information about finding a speech and language therapist working in the NHS or in private practice)

- Royal College of Speech and Language Therapists www.rcslt.org

- Association of Speech and Language Therapists in Independent Practice (ASLTIP) www.helpwithtalking.com

**Major charities** (which support people with communication difficulties and provide resources for parents and teachers)

- Afasic www.afasic.org.uk

- I CAN www.ican.org.uk

- The Autism Education Trust www.theautismeducationtrust.org.uk

- The Communications Trust www.thecommunicationstrust.org.uk

# 3 Phonological Awareness and Phonics

In an ideal world, all children should be able to benefit from exposure to high quality, systematic, structured phonic teaching, of the type recommended by Sir Jim Rose (2006) in his review of the teaching of early reading.

Children passing from the Early Years Foundation Stage (EYFS) to Key Stage 1 should have been comprehensively observed and informally assessed against the EYFS profile, so that those whose language and literacy development is falling behind, or differs significantly from that of their peers, will already be identified. It is generally acknowledged that the earlier a child is identified as 'at risk' for dyslexic type difficulties, the more effective targeted intervention will be.

# What you need to know

Phonological awareness and letter-knowledge are very good predictors of success in acquiring literacy. Children who have difficulties with phonological processing may be unable to access the primary curriculum.

## Phonological awareness

Phonological awareness can be defined as **the ability to identify and manipulate sounds within words**. This is an oral/aural skill and is *not* a part of reading and writing per se, but a precursor to it.

A Year 1 child with well-developed phonological skills would be able to:

- generate a rhyme, by offering the word *hat* to rhyme with *cat, mat, sat, fat;*
- identify the odd one out when hearing the words *pin, thin, cat* and *spin;*
- use alliteration, as when playing I-Spy, by reliably suggesting words which begin with the target phoneme (sound) – for example, *I Spy with my little eye something beginning with w… wall, window, washing, wasp, wellies;*
- blend and segment words orally, knowing that /m/a/t/ is blended together to give the word *mat* and that, conversely, the word *mat* can be segmented into its three phonemes /m/a/t/.

Teachers should be aware that segmenting and blending are reversible processes and children should practise these skills in tandem. Excellent materials to support the development of phonological awareness can be found in Aspects 4 to 7 of Phase One of *Letters and Sounds* (2007).

Speaking and Listening skills which incorporate all these features will have been introduced in the EYFS, but their delivery may have been too rapid for children who are at risk of dyslexia.

Phonological awareness is a cognitive skill and is distinct from knowledge about written letters (graphemes). Poor phonological skills mean that children will not be able to generalise from a known word (e.g. *look*) to an unknown word (e.g. *hook*) for reading, because of their inability to distinguish rhyming patterns. The same is true for spelling, since if you can spell *name* you can spell *game, same* and *tame* by analogy.

So the development of phonological awareness – which for most children precedes the learning of the alphabetic code – is a crucially important skill-set for the acquisition of literacy. Any impairment or delay in acquiring phonological awareness will be a compelling indicator for dyslexia.

# Phonic decoding

The next crucial element when assessing for possible dyslexia is that of **phonic knowledge**. Put simply, phonics relates to knowledge of the alphabetic code, together with blending and segmenting skills, and how to represent a phoneme (a sound heard) by its grapheme (its written representation).

The first problem for teachers of literacy is that the coding system requires us to represent the 44 speech sounds of the English language by combinations of the 26 letters of the alphabet. Phonic teaching also requires us to demonstrate how segmenting and blending phonemes underpin writing and reading.

Another tricky issue in connection with phonemic awareness, is the fact that letters can represent different phonemes, depending on whether they are 'hard' or 'soft'. For example, the *g* in *gun* is a hard /g/ sound whereas the *g* in *gym* is the soft /j/ sound. Similarly the grapheme *c* can be decoded as the hard /k/ in *cot,* or the soft sound /s/ in the word *city.*

For the dyslexic learner this variation between graphemes and phonemes is baffling and inconsistent. Because phonics is the main driving force for the acquisition of literacy, and children are encouraged to segment and blend the phonemes that they hear, they may reasonably wonder why *giant* can't be spelled **jiant**.

If you analyse the complexities of the letter–sound relationships in the words *sister, Cinderella, cat, kitten,* the /s/ sound in *sister* and *Cinderella,* is represented first by an *s* then by a *c*. The /k/ phoneme is represented by the letter *c* in *cat* but by *k* in *kitten*. When one examines this closely, it is surprising that most children do actually master reading and spelling as successfully as they do!

English is a language which quickly moves beyond regular cvc (consonant, vowel, consonant) words like *cat* and *dog*, to digraphs (two letters making a new sound) such as the *ea* in *meat, or* the *sh* in *shop.*

Of course the acquisition of literacy skills in English is made even more difficult for beginner readers and writers by the high number of exception words. Even high frequency words like *said*, used by Year 1 children, cannot be decoded using phonics and conforms to no specific word pattern.

**Context** also has a vital part to play, since you cannot successfully decode words like *tear* until you can decode the surrounding words. In the sentence *'she cried real tears'*, **tears** is decoded differently from the same word in the context *'The boy tears the paper off the present.'* (There is also the question of how to pronounce *present*, which is also context-dependent in this sentence!)

But more of this in Chapters 4 and 6, when we discuss reading for meaning and spelling in context.

Current national guidelines expect all children to know all of the letter names by the end of the Foundation Stage and to have passed through Phases 2 to 6 of *Letters and Sounds* (2007), or an equivalent phonics programme, by the end of Year 2. In other words, phonics teaching is time-limited and by the end of Key Stage 1 children should have mastered the decoding skills they need to become fluent readers.

For this reason it is vital that phonological awareness skills are systematically tested, for all children at the end of Reception, and again for children giving rise to concern, towards the end of Year 1. The teachers' guidance notes for *Letters and Sounds* state unequivocally:

*'Children's progress should be tracked through a reliable assessment process that identifies learning difficulties at an early stage. Children's letter knowledge and ability to segment and blend need to be assessed **individually**, as their actual attainment level may not be sufficiently well ascertained in group activities.'*

Appendix 4 of the *Letters and Sounds* Six-Phase Teaching Programme contains some useful assessment tasks on blending and segmentation as well as non-word reading. However, some additional phonological testing may be required to assess those skills which *precede* phoneme knowledge. We know that dyslexic children may not have mastered the simple grapheme/phoneme correspondences detailed in Phase 2 of *Letters and Sounds* as fast as their peers, so you could administer some or all of the measures outlined below to any primary-aged pupil about whom you have a concern. The informal assessment techniques and tests shown in Figure 3.1 may be used freely and the results might suggest dyslexic tendencies.

# Practical assessment

## Informal assessment

Phonological skills can be assessed through the simple and easy to administer oral tests set out in Figure 3.1. Although informal and therefore in no way standardised, these can shed light on areas of weakness in phonological processing which will be relatively straightforward to support and strengthen through focused teaching.

Remember that in testing phonological skills and phonic knowledge, you will need:

- a quiet and undisturbed environment, where the child can hear and attend freely;

- to undertake such screening on an individual, one-to-one basis, because these skills are tested **orally**: the child has no writing to do;

- to record the child's responses as well as noting how much effort he needed to give the response;

- a set of cards with the lowercase letters, one per card. You can show them in any order you choose, but the order followed here is that from *Letters and Sounds*, using the grid on pages 201 and 202.

Furthermore:

- discretion is needed in administering these tests with very young children: professional judgement is required about when to discontinue any given section;

- incorrect responses will be very useful in assessing the specific area of difficulty;

- rewards and stickers will be needed for engagement with the process;

- it would not be appropriate to use these tests beyond Key Stage 2.

By the end of all this testing you should have amassed a great deal of information. Always observe *how* the child attempted the tasks and note this down. For example:

- is there a swift, automatic response?

- does the child sub-vocalise/mutter repeatedly under his breath?

- is the eventual answer accurate or not?

You can construct a summary sheet of your findings, by using the record sheet shown in Figure 3.2.

# Formal assessment

Various commercial resources – such as the *Phonological Assessment Battery* (PhAB) (1997); the *Phonological Abilities Test* (PAT) (1997), and *Sound Linkage* (2000) – are available.

Each of these measures requires familiarity with the test protocols and a quiet, undisturbed setting in which to administer them orally. Specialist SpLD teachers and speech and language therapists may have some or all of the tests above, so it's worth asking if they are available in your setting.

Bear in mind that cost could be an issue when considering the purchase of commercial tests. It is worth noting that *Sound Linkage* offers both initial assessment procedures and a useful range of teaching support materials, so it serves two functions.

# INFORMAL TESTS OF PHONOLOGICAL SKILLS

## 1. Rhyme Detection skills

**Say:** *Do these pairs rhyme or are they different?*

Give a practice example (e.g. *dish/fish*). *Do they rhyme or are they different?*

| Test items | Responses |
|---|---|
| man/pan | |
| hit/nip | |
| tap/cap | |
| leg/beg | |
| fox/mix | |

## 2. Rhyme Generation skills

**Say:** *Now can you think of two words which rhyme with these words?*

Give a practice example (e.g. *bump; lump*); you could say *jump, dump*.

| Test items | Responses *(note and accept non-word attempts)* |
|---|---|
| fat, pat | |
| book, cook | |
| ring, bring | |
| land, hand | |
| will, still | |

## 3. Alliteration skills

**Say:** *What phoneme/sound begins all these groups of words?*

*Here's a practice one*: Happy Harry hates hairy hedgehogs.

*What phoneme/sound starts all these words?? Is it …/h/?*

*Now try these:*

| Test items | Responses |
|---|---|
| Monkey Mike munches meatballs … | |
| Laura loves little, laughing lambs … | |
| Pass Pippa's pudding … | |
| Robin Redbreast runs round … | |
| Suzie's soft, silky socks … | |

## 4. Phoneme Blending skills

**Say:** *I'm going to say some sounds; I want you to put the sounds together and tell me what word they make. Here's a practice one:/m/a/n/.*

NB: leave a one-second gap between each sound, and say each phoneme string *twice*.

| Test items | Responses |
|---|---|
| /l/e/g/…/l/e/g/ | |
| /s/u/n/ | |
| /ch/i/p/ | |
| /d/u/s/t/ | |
| /s/t/a/m/p/ | |

## 5. Phoneme Segmentation skills

**Say:** *Now I'm going to say some words and I want you to tell me which phonemes/sounds you can hear. Let's try one first.*

**Say:** *Dog, what sounds can you hear in dog? /d/o/g/… Very good!*

*Now try these* (say each word twice). Record the responses.

| Test items | Responses |
|---|---|
| cap | |
| zip | |
| sock | |
| vest | |
| gloves | |

## 6. Syllable Awareness

You will need to have a small ruler or hammer for this test. Demonstrate how to tap out the syllables. Practise twice with these words: *cat* = 1 tap; *bucket* = 2 taps (*buck–et*). You could also practise with the child's name, bearing in mind that each syllable needs to have a vowel sound in it.

**Say:** *Now you tap out the beats in these words for me:*

| Test items | Responses – *record the number of taps* |
|---|---|
| pig (1) | |
| jacket (2) | |
| ant (1) | |
| rabbit (2) | |
| Saturday (3) | |

## 7. Phoneme Deletion skills

**Say:** *Now this time I'm going to say a word and I want you to take off the first sound you hear. Let's practise one.*

**Say:** *Drip: let's take off the /d/… what is left? Yes, rip, that's right.* (You may need to repeat this with another trial, e.g. flip, so that the child understands what to do.)

*Now let's try these:*

| Test items | Responses |
|---|---|
| Bus; take off the first sound, leaves? *(us)* | |
| Jam; take off the first sound, leaves? *(am)* | |
| Hit; take off the first sound, leaves? *(it)* | |
| Stick; take off the first sound, leaves? *(tick)* | |
| Bread: take off the first sound, leaves? *(red)* | |

## 8. Non-word Reading

Photocopy the pupil's reading card on page 38.

**Say:** *Now this one is about reading the names of some funny creatures. Let's look at this funny creature. His name is* **vip**. *Now let's try these:*

| Test items | Responses |
|---|---|
| jem | |
| rak | |
| pof | |
| cug | |
| dremp | |

## 9. Grapheme/Phoneme Knowledge

Present your letter cards to the pupil in the order shown on the record sheet (Figure 3.2), and circle the ones the pupil does not know.

# Pupil's reading card

**Say:** *Here is a funny creature. His name is ...*

**vip**

*Now can you read these names?*

**jem**

**rak**

**pof**

**cug**

**dremp**

**Figure 3.1:** Informal tests of phonological skills

# PHONOLOGICAL SKILLS – SUMMARY

**Pupil's name:**             **Date tested/Age:**

| Skill assessed | Number of correct responses (out of 5) | Quality of responses *(mostly correct, mostly incorrect, fluently given, or effortful)* |
|---|---|---|
| 1. Rhyme Detection | | |
| 2. Rhyme Generation | | |
| 3. Alliteration | | |
| 4. Phoneme Blending | | |
| 5. Phoneme Segmentation | | |
| 6. Syllable Awareness | | |
| 7. Phoneme Deletion | | |
| 8. Non-word Reading | | |

**9. Grapheme/Phoneme Knowledge** *(circle those not known)*

| | | | | | |
|---|---|---|---|---|---|
| s | a | t | p | i | n |
| m | d | g | o | c | k |
| ck | e | u | r | h | b |
| f | l | j | v | w | x |
| y | z | qu | ch | sh | th |

Special Needs Language & Literacy Assessment Handbook: photocopy master

**Figure 3.2:** Informal test of phonological skills – summary of results

# What next?

Your completed record sheet (Figure 3.2) should give you plenty of specific information about a particular child's strengths and weaknesses. Remember that these findings will need to be interpreted with caution, taking into account the pupil's age, stage, context, home circumstances and access to previous high quality teaching.

The EYFS and Key Stage 1 are the optimal times to plan focused intervention and support for phonological and phonemic skills training. There is a large body of research evidence to show that interventions are most effective if delivered well before the age of 7–8 years.

However, we need to remember that some dyslexic children will have been taught phonics and even more phonics! Whilst Jim Rose (2009) asserts that *'high-quality, systematic phonics should be the prime approach for teaching children to read'*, some dyslexic children will rarely master all the necessary phonic skills, so they must learn to read through different channels.

However, as Rose also states in his independent report, *'… it is important to acknowledge that some children with dyslexia can respond very slowly even to high quality teaching approaches.'*

There is rarely much point in concentrating on phonic skills in Key Stages 3 and 4, since by now other more pressing literacy issues will need addressing. This will be the focus of Chapter 8.

So to give some pointers for teaching a child in **Reception**:

- If he knows most of the grapheme–phoneme (letter–sound) correspondences, but cannot segment and blend reliably, then this would be the priority area to work on.

- Use of puppets, tactile 3D objects, rhyming songs, jingles and plastic letters would be most effective in developing knowledge about phonemes, and for securing blending and segmentation skills.

An excellent resource which gets right to the heart of phonological skills training is Liz Baldwin's *I Hear with my Little Ear* (2006). This resource includes 101 interactive games addressing syllables, initial and final sounds, rhyming, phoneme manipulation and photocopiable resources. The games can be delivered by a teaching assistant (TA) and used in group situations, for those children exhibiting difficulties with phonological awareness and early phonics.

Other activities to support the development of phonological and phonic skills could be taken from *Letters and Sounds* Phases 2 to 6: from *Jolly Phonics; Read Write Inc; Sound Linkage; SmartKids* materials, or any number of other commercially published schemes.

If we now consider a **9 year old**, with age-appropriate English language skills, good school attendance and good teaching, but who is still unable to rhyme, segment and blend, or manipulate phonemes successfully, this evidence would be highly significant. Assessment by a specialist, leading to a planned programme of intervention, would be needed.

> **Remember that all materials should be age-appropriate. It would be counter-productive to work with a 10 year old, using materials suited to a Reception child, even if that is the right level of difficulty: try to match interest level also.**

Informal testing, such as that described above, corresponds to the Level 2 Skills assessment, outlined in the Rose Report (2009), which should pave the way for more comprehensive assessment by a specialist teacher (a teacher with a postgraduate qualification in the assessment and teaching of pupils with specific learning difficulties), and specific intervention if needed.

The class or subject teacher should already be using personalised learning, which tailors teaching and learning to the needs of the individual pupil, so that evidence gathered through Assessment for Learning (AfL) and Assessing Pupils' Progress (APP) is already available.

## The solution to a common problem

Dyslexic pupils may be unable to choose from the range of alternative graphemic representations of the long /a/ sound as in *play, make, rain, eight, acorn, they*. In each of the six examples just listed, the long /a/ sound is represented by different groups of letters. For the dyslexic child, who may have been well taught about the possible common ways to represent the long /a/, the problem will be which version to choose from: is it *ay*, *ai* or *a_e* which is needed to spell the word *cave*? A **word family** approach will be the most helpful – see Chapter 6.

There may of course be a host of other reasons why a child fails to acquire age-appropriate literacy skills, apart from dyslexia. These might include more generalised (global) learning difficulties, or sensory, physical, emotional or social factors. Jim Rose recommends an *'evaluation of possible co-occurring difficulties... and discussion with all concerned'* and this is certainly the right course of action.

So, if your focused interventions tailored to the needs of the pupil have not resulted in significant progress within two terms, the next step would be to refer the pupil to a specialist dyslexia teacher, or educational psychologist. They will have the specialist skills needed to make a full diagnosis. The information you provide about assessment and intervention already undertaken, will be crucial in this process, together with information about the pupil's responses to reading and spelling instruction. We will find out more about these aspects of literacy in the next two chapters.

## Summary of actions and key points

■ Check oral phonological skills first and note results using summary sheet Figure 3.2.

■ Check grapheme/phoneme (letter/sound) knowledge.

■ When articulating single consonant sounds (e.g. /m/), keep the sound as pure as possible (e.g. *mmm…*), resisting the temptation to put an *uhh* sound at the end (e.g. *muh)*.

■ Check that alphabet friezes or classroom displays do not confuse letter names and sounds. Inconsistent messages may inadvertently be given by Early Years practitioners, when they link a picture of an ice-cream with the short vowel /i/ (as in *insect*); or an orange *and* an owl to illustrate the short vowel /o/.

■ When testing or teaching letter/sound knowledge, remember that it's the letter *sound*, **not its name**, which is relevant for phonics teaching.

■ Make all teaching oral and interactive, using vocabulary within the pupil's understanding.

■ When covering phonic patterns (word families), use colour to highlight the common pattern.

■ Work on words containing the same phonic pattern within real, meaningful sentences (*not* unconnected word lists), as this will enable the words to be remembered in context.

■ Know when to refer onwards to a specialist professional.

# 4  Reading

The teaching of reading has always been viewed as a contentious and somewhat political issue. This debate has focused primarily on the most effective method of teaching reading. We must remember that *most* children learn to read successfully, whatever method is in fashion, and despite the vagaries of English orthography (spelling), which some people consider to be responsible for poor levels of literacy.

Let us look briefly at the progress made in the understanding of how beginner readers learn to read.

Long ago children were taught reading by rote – that is, they all chanted aloud together from a text displayed by the teacher, who held a pointer, to demonstrate the reading direction, a bit like using karaoke machines today. In this type of instruction, memorisation and repetition played a significant part.

In the 1950s, reading schemes such as *Kitty and Rover* were used. These relied on the use of a small selection of sight words which had to be memorised from flash cards, followed by the oral recital of phonic word lists such as *feet, meet, sheet, beet*, where some of the words were quite beyond the understanding of the average five year old. This was phonic drilling at the expense of meaning.

Then came *Look and Say*, where children were taught whole words in Reception and expected to memorise these by the visual shape of the words. This worked well with words like *aeroplane* from the *Janet and John* series, but proved much more problematical with words like *horse* and *house*, which visually are very similar. Children had word cards which they had to memorise and they would not be given the next reading book until the new words were firmly committed to memory. So progress through the scheme was dishearteningly slow for poor readers.

This put a huge strain on visual memory, until it was discovered that there was a finite limit to the number of words which could be memorised like this. When you consider the repetitive content of early primers such as:

*'Look, Janet, look, look! Janet, look up. Look up, Janet, look up!'*

you can see the shortcomings, in terms of engagement and motivation!

Then came *Language Experience*, or 'Real Books', which was a reaction against the memorising of single words and dull, phonic drilling.

Language experience encouraged children to explore exciting and colourful books which enthusiastic adults would read to them. The idea was that children would discover that reading was truly enjoyable and they would want to become proficient at it. Children were encouraged to choose texts themselves from banded book shelves – with the result that reading from scheme books was discontinued.

This was very motivating for good beginner readers, but not so helpful for those who needed formal instruction about how to decode print. Language experience gave rise to poor readers who were *'barking at print'* – that is memorising whole books, without understanding – because they lacked the instructional tools to decode new words in unfamiliar contexts.

We can learn much from these initiatives when dealing with the difficulties presented by struggling readers in today's schools, who fail to engage with reading and/or lack fluency.

## What you need to know

The Rose Review (2006) on the teaching of Early Reading advocated the **Simple View of Reading**. This was already very familiar to specialist dyslexia teachers, and was described by Hoover and Gough in 1990.

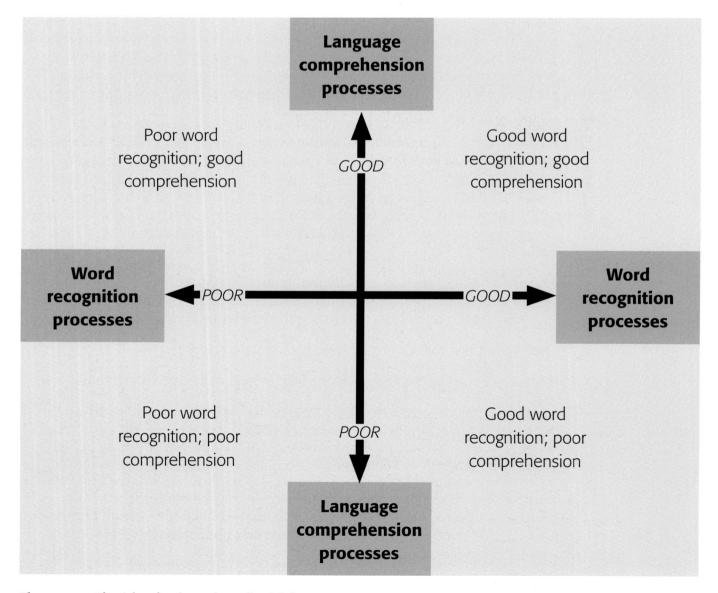

**Figure 4.1:** The 'simple view of reading' (after Rose, 2009)

Essentially, the 'simple view of reading' recognises that there are two distinct dimensions to reading:

- word recognition
- language comprehension

These equate to the *decoding* aspects (word recognition) and the *meaning* aspects (language comprehension). This two-dimensional model acknowledges that **both** decoding and comprehension are vital for learning to read and for understanding what is read.

Many dyslexics would fall within the top-left quadrant of this diagram; that is, they would exhibit good comprehension skills, but possess poor word recognition skills. So if someone else read a text to them, they would understand it well enough. But if they had to read the text themselves, poor word-attack and weak decoding skills would prevent them from getting to the meaning.

When considering the teaching of reading, it is as well to keep some basic facts in mind:

*1* *Most* children learn to read whatever the method – and sometimes *despite* the teacher's best efforts or preferred teaching methods.

*2* A proportion of children will have significant and persistent difficulties acquiring literacy *whatever* the prevailing method.

*3* As Jim Rose (2009) reminds us, *'failure to read is often to do with the nature of the teaching rather than the nature of the child.'*

*4* Good readers become more proficient by continual and increasingly successful interaction with texts. However, poor readers make little progress because the books they can access offer limited vocabulary and content: such children tend to avoid reading.

Generally speaking, therefore, *good* readers progress rapidly through graded reading books, derive enjoyment from text, and go on to choose books on topics which interest them, whether fiction or information texts. In this way they interact with text even more and derive enjoyment, praise and encouragement from adults for their good literacy skills.

*Poor* readers, on the other hand, are stuck on books which may not be very interesting and all too often are inappropriately childish. They avoid reading whenever possible, since it is not a pleasurable activity and they do not want to be seen as stuck on 'babyish' texts. So, they interact with text less – and the gap between good and poor readers becomes wider over time. This is sometimes known as the *Matthew Effect* (see page 65).

The *nature* of the teaching, as quoted by Rose, should include insightful, intuitive responses to the child, starting from where he is – not by forcing him through a specific programme, however effective it seems to be for most children.

The Inclusion statement enshrined within the National Curriculum allows for *'considerable flexibility in how it can be delivered.'* This gives teachers more scope for responding to individual needs than they might have supposed.

Current national guidelines assert that in the Foundation Stage and Key Stage 1 – whilst both word recognition and language comprehension are crucially interlinked and important – it is the *word recognition (decoding)* aspects which should be the focus of instruction for beginner readers. There is an emphasis on moving from *learning to read* in the Foundation Stage and Key Stage 1 towards *reading to learn* at the beginning of Key Stage 2.

It is fair to say that every primary school teacher would agree with this proposition, because you have to be able to decode before you can understand. But sometimes the effort involved in decoding text is so great, that not only is comprehension impaired, but the child shows frustration with the immediate task – and reluctance to read becomes the norm.

Children have to *want* to engage with the literacy process; they have to derive something personally significant from text, or they will fail to engage with it. And we know that demotivated young readers who are turned off from the whole reading process are extremely difficult to re-engage later on.

For children at risk of literacy difficulties, 'meaning-getting' is as important – if not more so – than decoding, which may continue to be weak. Many children already identified will have been well-drilled in phonics and will still struggle to read, so phonic teaching is not a universal panacea.

# Practical assessment of reading

There is a wide range of reading tests available from the three main UK publishers – Hodder Education, Pearson, GL Assessment – which vary widely in terms of cost, the time taken to administer and mark them, their focus and thus the information they provide. Some tests can be completed in ten minutes, whilst others need half an hour or more. There are tests for group/whole-class use and others for individual administration; some are available in on-screen interactive (single user or networkable) versions. The cost – initial purchase price plus 'consumable' record sheets – and time needed for administration and marking, must all be weighed up in relation to the value and scope of the information gained.

We now look at some widely used tests, with their benefits and possible drawbacks. Other tests can be evaluated using similar criteria, bearing in mind the particular needs of your own working context.

It is to be hoped that all assessments will lead to some appropriately focused learning support, but in some contexts the main need is to identify the children whose reading skills are so weak that they need TA support in class, and extra time and/or a reader in examinations.

The difference between pencil and paper and oral tests, as well as being highly pertinent in terms of staff time, is also fundamental from the pupil's perspective. Due to intellectual factors as well as emotional ones, some pupils with dyslexia will find it much harder to cope with reading aloud than to demonstrate their understanding of written material by reading the text to themselves and then using a pencil.

Nevertheless, if setting IEP targets is your goal, you will learn more about the pupil's needs from a one-to-one assessment session where you hear him read and can talk to him. However, if you need to find out who is eligible for exam arrangements, a group-reading pencil and paper test – where the task closely mirrors the exam setting – may be more suitable, as well as a more efficient use of your time.

# Oral (individual) reading tests

These all require you to hear a pupil read aloud and record his responses. They also give the opportunity to make notes about his strategies and discuss his difficulties with him. They range from brief graded single-word tests to lengthier prose reading tests that may assess accuracy, fluency (speed of reading) and/or comprehension. An example of each is described below.

Test catalogues and online examples will enable you to select tests with suitable content for your own school.

## Hodder Oral Reading Tests
(Vincent, D. & Crumpler, M., 2006, Hodder Education)

**Age range:** 5–16+

**Time allowed:** 2–3 minutes per test.

**Parallel forms?** Yes

### What does it measure?

1. Accuracy of single-word reading (untimed).
2. Speed of reading single cvc words (a separate and optional test).
3. Accuracy when reading sentences (a separate and optional test).

### Advantages

■ Using the sentence reading test, an opportunity exists to gauge how well the pupil makes use of context cues to aid decoding. If his score on this section is significantly higher than his score on the single-word section, it is likely that he is making good use of context cues.

■ The single-word reading test can be used to assess eligibility for assistance during exams (although the speed of reading test does not meet the criteria for extra time).

### Disadvantage

■ It does not measure reading comprehension at continuous text level.

## Diagnostic Reading Analysis, 2nd edition
(Crumpler, M. & McCarty, C., 2008, Hodder Education)

**Age range:** 7–16

**Time needed:** about 15 minutes.

**Parallel forms?** Yes

### What does it measure?

1. Listening comprehension.
2. Reading accuracy (at text level).
3. Speed of reading at text level.
4. Comprehension of text.
5. Comprehension processing speed.

### Advantages

■ This test takes listening comprehension into account when deciding where to start.

■ In general, a pupil will only have to read three passages in order to produce a reliable result.

■ The **DRA** is designed to suit weaker readers.

■ It can be used to assess eligibility for extra time during exams.

■ The tester does not assist the pupil (e.g. give words) and therefore a true measure of independent reading ability is obtained . (This contrasts with the *Neale Analysis of Reading Ability*, where the teacher gives unknown words to the pupil.)

■ An optional CD-ROM is also available which enables a detailed diagnostic report to be produced for each pupil, with suggestions for appropriate learning support.

### Disadvantages

■ This test takes time and practice to administer.

■ It does not give information about accuracy/automaticity of single-word recognition, since the pupil might be making excellent use of context cues (illustrations, his own knowledge, the storyline) to help him decode words through prediction.

*    *    *

If you are not sure where to start in a phonics programme, a **nonword reading test** is a very useful diagnostic tool. For Key Stage 1, an informal test (see page 32) might be used to check out decoding skills. But for Key Stages 2–4, where a 'patchy' grasp of more advanced and complex phonics may be the chief problem, a commercially produced test could prove an extremely useful resource.

## Nonword Reading Test
(Crumpler, M. & McCarty, C., 2004, Hodder Education)

**Age range:** 6–16+

**Time needed:** 5–10 minutes.

**Parallel forms?** Yes

### What does it measure?

1. Accuracy of phonological decoding skills.

2. Speed of nonword reading.

### Advantages

■ A pupil with a good *sight vocabulary* might do reasonably well on a graded single-word reading test, but actually have quite weak decoding skills which this test will certainly reveal. (Nonwords cannot have been read before and become known by sight.)

■ The record sheet provides a means of analysing where the gaps in his knowledge are – vowel digraphs, final blends, syllabic structure and so on. The manual contains a useful chapter on how to use test results to plan learning support and choose IEP targets.

■ The test could be used as additional evidence of the need for extra time during exams.

### Disadvantages

■ It requires practice on the part of the tester – the record form is quite dense.

■ It does not assess the pupil's reading comprehension skills or sight vocabulary.

# Silent reading tests

These are pencil and paper tests (which may also be available as on-screen tests) and can be used with individuals, small or large groups or whole classes for screening purposes. Administered to a whole class, the results will enable the teacher to identify pupils who need a more detailed investigation of their reading skills. Or they can be used with a group of children already causing concern. Silent reading tests range from those which are quick to administer and focus on individual word recognition (e.g. *Wordchains*) to fairly lengthy tests which cover a wider range of reading strategies, including vocabulary knowledge and comprehension, such as the *Access Reading Test* (see below).

## Wordchains
(Miller Guron, L., 1999, GL Assessment)

**Age range:** 7–adult

**Time taken:** 6 minutes.

No parallel forms

This easy-to-administer test must be carefully timed, as it focuses on speed as well as accuracy of *word recognition*. Strings of three and four common words are shown with no spaces between them (e.g. *sandcoffeeblue*). The pupils must mark where the boundaries between the words are, as quickly as possible. This section is preceded by another called *Letterchains*, requiring a similar approach but where the stimuli are strings of letters (e.g. *kkkttttbbbb*). This primes them for the second section and enables their visual identification skills and eye–hand co-ordination to be checked without involving any word recognition. So long as the score is normal on *Letterchains*, a poor score on the *Wordchains* section would flag up the need for further investigation.

### Advantages

- It takes very little time to administer and is easy to mark.

- It quickly identifies children with poor word recognition who may be dyslexic.

- This test also flags up children who may need further assessment if their scores on *both* sections of the test fall below average.

- It can be used to screen for pupils who might need access arrangements during exams.

### Disadvantage

- No aspect of reading comprehension is assessed. Therefore those whose word recognition skills are fine but have problems with language comprehension processes would not be identified.

## Hodder Group Reading Tests 1–3, 2nd edition
(Vincent, D. & Crumpler, M., 2007, Hodder Education)

**Age range: Test 1** ages 5:0 to 9:0 (Years 1 to 3); **Test 2** ages 7:0 to 12:0 (Years 2 to 6); **Test 3** ages 9:5 to 16+ (Years 5 to 11)

**Time taken:** 30 minutes.

**Parallel forms?** Yes

Available in pencil and paper and on-screen versions.

The **Hodder Group Reading Tests 1–3** assess pupils' reading at word, sentence and text levels.

### Advantages

- These are 'wide-range' tests, so are suitable for pupils of varied reading abilities, from well below to above average for their age group.

- Results are given as standardised scores, reading ages and national curriculum levels.

- **HGRT 2** and **3** can be used to assess eligibility for 'access arrangements' at Key Stage 2 and GCSE (the on-screen interactive version includes the facility to compare assessments with and without extra time automatically).

■ A *Scorer/Profiler CD-ROM* is available separately to automate score conversions, analyse and interpret group performance data, and track individual pupil progress.

**Disadvantages**

■ Each test gives one 'global' score and so specific difficulties with, say, *comprehension* at text level compared to single-word reading *accuracy* are not separated out.

■ The correlation between the results pupils obtain on **HRGT 1** and **2** and the National Curriculum levels they obtain during Key Stage 1 and 2 statutory tests is 'moderate' rather than high. A follow-up individual assessment of reading may be warranted in some cases.

## Access Reading Test

(McCarty, C. & Crumpler, M., 2006, Hodder Education)

**Age range:** 7–20+

**Time allowed:** 30 minutes (many children will complete in less time). This test may also be re-scored after 25% extra time has been allowed, to see if an application for extra time during examinations may be appropriate.

Interactive single-user and networkable versions are also available, and include the facility to compare assessments with and without extra time automatically.

**Parallel forms?** Yes

The **ART** assesses four aspects of reading skill:

1. Literal comprehension (information from instructions and factual accounts).

2. Vocabulary knowledge.

3. Comprehension requiring inference, prediction or opinion.

4. Comprehension requiring analysis (agree/disagree/does not say).

**Advantages**

■ This is a 'wide range' test, suitable for all levels of reading ability.

■ It gives the results as standardised scores, reading ages and percentiles.

■ A profile of strengths and weaknesses is available: the four subtest scores can be compared to the averages for boys or girls for each age group, and learning support can then be targeted to the greatest area of need.

■ It can be used to assess eligibility for extra time during exams.

**Disadvantage**

■ Low scores may be due to poor reading accuracy rather than deficits in comprehension or vocabulary per se. Individual assessment of single-word reading will also be needed to ascertain the exact nature of the problem.

## Informal assessment of reading strategies and skills

If you already know that a child is a reluctant reader and having difficulties, and are more interested in working out just what you could do to boost his skills without necessarily using a formal test, a very useful informal technique is described below. It is very similar to the **miscue analysis** methodology first advocated by Marie Clay (1972).

1   Ask the child's teacher to select a reading book with which he is not familiar and will be *slightly* too difficult for him (rather than well within his capacities). This is because you need him to make sufficient errors for you to analyse – about 20 is ideal.

2   Photocopy a page or two (depending on the age of the child) some way into a chapter to function as a record sheet for yourself and attach it to your clipboard.

3   Introduce the task to the child (*'I'd like you to read some of this to me. I'm not going to help you, as I want to see how you get on by yourself. I'll start off and then you can read some to me ...'*). Reassure him about potential mistakes/failure.

4   Read enough of the book/chapter to get an idea of what it is all about, then invite the child to read the next section to you (which you have already photocopied).

5   As he reads, discreetly mark your copy, ticking words correctly read and underlining/crossing out words he misreads or refuses. It is *very important* to make some attempt to record what he actually says when he makes a mistake. It doesn't matter how you do this, so long as you can understand it afterwards. For example, if he sounds out a word successfully, put a wiggly line underneath and write *s–o* above. If he misreads *house* as *horse*, cross it out and write *horse* above. Mark in refusals, omissions and insertions. This does take practice but it is well worth doing.

6   When you have a good sample of errors (about 20) finish the chapter/section for or with him. Ask the pupil how he felt about the experience, whether he reads at home or with anyone else, whether he has been taught strategy checking (see below) and conclude the session in a reassuring way.

## Analysing the results

This is not an exact science, but it is often possible to see quite clearly that a pupil's main difficulties lie in problems with one strategy or another by analysing the results as follows:

■ Out of the total number of errors, how many are clearly due to decoding difficulties – for example refusals and misread words such as *house* for *horse*, *who* for *which*, etc? Say there are 4 refusals and 12 misread words. Of these 16, how many really altered the meaning to the extent that comprehension was impaired and/or the sentence uttered was completely ungrammatical – for example: *horse* for *house*, *kitten* for *kite* (but **not** *who* for *which*)? Say this is 12/16 (i.e. 75%). This will show you that the pupil is so locked into a phonic approach (even though he is not at all proficient) that he is making little or no effort to engage with the text and make some sense of it. This child not only needs more instruction on decoding skills, but also *strategies* (see page 60).

■ If on the other hand a bright youngster, by looking at the illustration, or gleaning the subject matter from the context, substituted *rabbits* for *hares*, or *frogs* for *toads*, or inserted or omitted words to make the sentence sound like normal language, it would be clear that he is making strenuous efforts to **read for meaning** even though his decoding skills are weak. Although this might result in him completely misunderstanding the passage, the point is that he is trying very hard to 'read for meaning'.

This child (like Jack, see Figure 4.2) will need more emphasis on accurate decoding – especially breaking words into syllables and checking the ends as well as beginnings of words.

### Example

Jack (Year 2) attempted the non-fiction 2 passage from Form B of the *Diagnostic Reading Analysis*. The accompanying colour illustration shows two rodents on lots of pieces of paper and some straw.

Rats can make good pets,
but you must look after them.

They need food, and clean water
to drink.

They like playing in their cage.

**Figure 4.2a:** The reading text

After carefully looking at the illustration, Jack read:

*'Mice make good pets but you must look a . . . a fuh . . . tuh . . . (refused) them. They need the right food and clean water. They like paper in their box.'*

Rats can make good pets,

but you must look after them.

They need food and clean water to drink.

They like playing in their cage.

**Figure 4.2b:** Jack's reading recorded

His response was analysed as shown in Figure 4.2c.

| Target | Response | Cues used | | |
|--------|----------|-----------|---|---|
| | | *Phonics* | *Context* | *Grammar* |
| 1. Rats | *Mice* | No | Yes | Yes |
| 2. Can | (omitted) | No | | Yes |
| 3. After | sounded out *a/f/t/* then refused | unsuccessful | | |
| 4. – | inserted *'the right'* | | Yes | Yes |
| 5. to drink | omitted | No | | |
| 6. playing | *paper* | Initial letter | Yes | Yes |
| 7. cage | *box* | No | Yes | Yes |

**Figure 4.2c:** Jack's reading analysed

It is quite clear that Jack does not decode accurately, but relies heavily on context cues, his own intelligence and good grammar to make very plausible-sounding attempts. He also inserted *'the right'* and omitted *'to drink'* which did not really affect the meaning of the passage. Whilst reading for meaning is very pleasing, Jack is severely at risk of failing to access the curriculum, since his accuracy is so poor. On a single-word reading test, his result was in the bottom 5% for his age. When there was no context to help him, he could not guess what the words were.

# READING ASSESSMENT – SUMMARY

**Pupil's name:**                               **Date of birth:**

**Age/School Year:**

**Summary completed by:**                   **Date:**

| **Test results**<br>Test used | Date | Tested by | Stand. Score/ Rdg Age | Grade (*average/ below/ above*) |
|---|---|---|---|---|
| | | | | |
| | | | | |
| | | | | |

| **Does he/she read at home?**<br><br>With/without support from family member/carer?<br><br>How often? | |
|---|---|
| Favourite reading material (if any) | |

| **Can he/she read:**<br>■ notes on board?<br>■ computer screen?<br>■ worksheets?<br>■ text books?<br>■ maths and exam questions? | (*specify particular problems here*) |
|---|---|
| **Decoding skills** are:<br>good/effortful/poor | (*specify problem areas*) |

| | |
|---|---|
| **Needs support with:**<br><br>■ individual letters<br><br>■ cvc words<br><br>■ consonant digraphs<br><br>■ vowel digraphs<br><br>■ common endings<br><br>■ syllable division<br><br>■ high-frequency words<br><br>■ subject vocabulary | |
| **Uses context:**<br>well/sometimes/never<br><br>**Needs to learn to use:**<br><br>■ illustrations/meaning at text level<br><br>■ own prior knowledge<br><br>■ grammatical cues | *(specify targets here)* |
| *Following meeting on:*<br><br>date<br><br>with<br><br>**Agreed actions:**<br><br>Review date agreed | *(transfer targets to IEP)* |
| **Re-test results**<br>Test used | Date     Tested by     Stand.<br>Score/<br>Rdg Age     Grade<br>*(average/<br>below/<br>above)* |

Special Needs Language & Literacy Assessment Handbook: photocopy master

**Figure 4.3:** Summary of reading assessment results

## Key points

■ Analyse your findings from information obtained from the pupil, his teachers and parents, your formal and/or informal test results and consider where the pupil's priority needs are.

For example, does he need further support in any of the following areas?
■ basic phonics
■ recognition of common letter strings
■ reading strategies
■ increased exposure to print
■ accessing suitable books
(See Chapter 5 for guidance on teaching methods.)

■ Prepare a brief summary (e.g. Figure 4.3) for use when discussing his needs with support staff and other adults.

■ Arrange to meet the staff involved, the pupil and his parents to discuss your findings and plan a support strategy.

■ Formulate his IEP and ensure appropriate resources are available.

■ If appropriate, refer the pupil to SENSS team, educational psychologist or other professionals.

■ If necessary, record the pupil's potential need for access arrangements during school tests and examinations, Key Stage 2 National Tests or public examinations (see Chapter 9).

# 5 Common Reading Problems . . . and some solutions

## Problem 1: Non-reader; no engagement with books
## Solution: Book-making

A small number of pupils will have very low scores indeed on reading tests. Both authors of this handbook have had extensive success in motivating and successfully teaching a range of pupils who would be classed as non-readers. The technique of constructing an *'own book'* has consistently been found to be the most appealing and motivating to kick-start emergent reading.

Book-making is much more accessible nowadays using digital images and computer software, but essentially the *'own book'* must be about the child himself or whatever he wants to read about. It should contain very simple sentences, using high-frequency words and significant words personal to the child, such as his own name and that of siblings, friends, pets and any particular hobby or preoccupation.

Each page should have one sentence of text and a photograph or picture. Personal books can have as few as four pages and should be laminated or carefully produced to give pride and ownership to the child, who will want to share this with his family. Whatever the child *wants* the book to be about is of paramount significance, so hobbies, football teams, family members, friends, personal collections can all become the topic of *'own books'*.

Where *own books* are memorable and relevant to a particular child and can be read and re-read to a variety of listeners, there is a very good chance that sight and personal words will be committed to long-term memory. From this re-reading of simple, meaningful sentences will come the cutting up and re-ordering of the sentences, much favoured by Marie Clay (1972) in her effective Reading Recovery programme.

## Problem 2: Poor single-word decoding
## Solution: Single-letter sounds and multi-sensory teaching

If a child exhibits poor decoding at the single-word level, then an analysis of errors should reveal if grapheme–phoneme correspondence is secure.

For example, if *b* and *p* are confused, so that *bat* is read as *pat*, then work on securing these graphemes is essential. This will need to be done in a multi-sensory, meaningful way, using tactile materials such as plastic letters, objects and toys.

**Multi-sensory teaching** is championed by teachers everywhere, and rightly so. But there are misunderstandings about what is involved. Multi-sensory teaching means seeing it, hearing it and actually doing it in an active way.

We do not need to be concerned with ascertaining preferred 'learning styles' and working exclusively with one sensory modality. We *all* use a range of sensory channels to learn, and the more ways of learning we can utilise, the better. So tracing individual graphemes on paper, in sand or flour is fine, as long as the child is encouraged to articulate the phoneme being written at the same time.

Walking a child in the writing direction along a huge chalked /p/ in the playground, whilst saying the letter sound, is a truly multi-sensory experience! Multi-sensory teaching, by its very nature, encompasses both reading and spelling, and this link should be reinforced at all times – so for more on multi-sensory teaching, see Chapter 7.

## Problem 3: Sounding out letter by letter
## Solution: Reading by analogy – onset and rime

Some children rely too heavily on their phonic knowledge, and their only strategy is to sound out letter by letter. The solution to this problem is to work through writing rather than reading, and to emphasise spelling patterns and common letter strings. Many English words conform to a regular pattern and if children are taught to identify these patterns in their spelling, then they will recognise them in their reading.

For information on teaching using **onset and rime**, see Chapter 7 on Writing.

## Problem 4: Poor comprehension
## Solution: Strategy checks (reading for meaning)

Strategy Checks will be familiar to teachers from the now superseded National Literacy Strategy. Children can easily be taught what to do if they encounter an unfamiliar word by using these ten prompts.

- What phoneme/sound does it begin with?
- What phoneme/sound does it end with?
- Can I sound it out?
- Can I break it up into syllables?
- Does it look like a word pattern that I know already?
- Can I read on and try the rest of the sentence?
- Can I re-read by going back and saying the phrase/line again?
- Can I look at the pictures/illustrations for a clue?
- Does what I read make good sense?
- Can I make a guess?

In this way a child is being taught to self-monitor – which is ultimately much more effective than just being told the word.

Some children have so much trouble with reading that they don't *expect* text to make sense at all. There could be many reasons for an inability to understand text.

Some of the ten prompts in the Strategy Check above will usefully serve to develop comprehension, so select those to do with meaning as opposed to phonics.

The given text might simply be too hard for the child – that is, at 'frustration level' (where he makes more than 10% of errors on a page) – and so changing to a less dense or easier text will enable the child to comprehend what he reads.

If prose reading is accurate and fluent, but questions on the passage read indicate a real lack of understanding, then further investigation would be warranted, from a speech and language therapist or educational psychologist to investigate specific language impairment, global learning difficulties, or other causal factors.

## Problem 5: Dislike and avoidance of reading
## Solution: Paired reading

The value of paired reading cannot be over-estimated. We know that poor readers interact with text less frequently than proficient readers. The goal is to improve fluency and skill through much increased exposure to print.

In today's busy classrooms, children are more likely to engage in guided or group reading than reading individually to a teacher. For good readers this is not an issue, but for poor or struggling readers they need one-to-one reading opportunities. This is good for the child's fragile self-esteem and provides the best opportunity for observational assessment and monitoring by a professional.

Paired reading, or 'buddy reading' as it is sometimes called, is easy to set up, and can be done by teaching assistants, volunteers, older children within the school or indeed at home. Both authors of this text have taught it successfully to teaching assistants, parents and older children and there is evidence that it works because it happens regularly for a short space of time, and is stress-free.

In paired reading there should be *no teaching* involved and the experience should be enjoyable for both parties. By choosing older children as tutors – such as challenging Year 6 boys as paired readers for younger struggling boys in Year 4 – both tutors and tutees gain in equal measure from the experience.

The underlying premise for paired reading, as described by Keith Topping (1995), is that repetition and practice are the key to increasing the sight vocabulary stored in long-term memory.

We therefore advocate the training of TransAge volunteers, involving teaching assistants and parents and carers, through simple workshops and by paired

# PAIRED READING – HOW TO DO IT

**1**    Ask the child's teacher to help him/her choose enjoyable books which he/she can nearly read without help. There should only be two or three words on each page that he/she does not know.

**2**    Agree with the child that you will read together for 10 minutes each day **for the next 6 weeks**. (Bribe him/her if necessary!)

**3**    Thumb through the book to get the gist of it.

*Start reading …*

**4**    Read a small amount aloud to the child.

**5**    Read the **same** section with the child joining in.

**6**    Now, the child should read the **same** section aloud to you.

*(4, 5 & 6 may be replaced by the tutor and the more competent child taking turns to read to each other.)*

**7**    If he/she hesitates for too long, or makes a mistake, say the right word straight away. Do NOT ask him/her to 'sound it out'.

**8**    Talk about the story now and then: ask the child if he/she can guess what is going to happen next …, why so-and-so said that…, etc.

*PRAISE the child for trying.*
*Be POSITIVE: stay CALM.*

- Note what has been done in the child's reading record.

- Make sure his/her teacher knows what you are doing and praises him/her too.

- If the child wants to read the same book again – that is fine – but try to encourage him/her to start another as well.

- **Do not give up!!!**

Special Needs Language & Literacy Assessment Handbook: photocopy master

**Figure 5.1:** Paired reading – how to do it

reading schemes using peer tutors, set up in schools by the SENCO or literacy coordinator.

The following section describes in some detail the theory and practice of this technique. Figure 5.1 provides simple instructions for paired reading 'tutors'.

The ultimate goal is for children to be fluent, accurate and motivated readers by the start of Key Stage 2 or as soon as practicable!

# Paired reading

Reading is a complex skill and the *only* way to improve it is by regular practice. When a child's reading does not improve steadily, the daily reading routine becomes an unwelcome chore, often leading to high levels of frustration and anxiety for all concerned. *Paired Reading* is a well-proven method of promoting reading skill in a stress-free way.

## The theory

Skilled readers recognise a very large proportion of the words they encounter in print. These make up their **sight vocabulary**. The beginning reader may have a sight vocabulary of just five or six words, whereas the mature reader will recognise tens of thousands. How does the size of the sight vocabulary increase? For each word encountered, but not recognised, the reader may:

■ use *phonics* to try and sound it out; and/or

■ guess/predict what it is *likely* to be: this is called *reading for meaning;*

■ be told the word by a helper: this method is called *Look and Say*.

The first two strategies may or may not be successful. They interrupt the flow of the reading and the sense of the text may be lost. The third method, however, is *always* successful – assuming the helper is an accurate reader!

Paired Reading builds up the *sight vocabulary* by the *Look and Say* method. This often also brings considerable gains in confidence and lessening of anxiety about reading.

## The method

*1* Choose a well-illustrated book – fact or fiction. Make sure it is written in language that the child understands. Ideally, he should be able to read 90–95% of the text unaided, but where reading ability does not match age/interest level, this can be difficult. It is vital that the child **enjoys** the book, so it is usually better to choose one that is interesting or funny, but a little too hard, than one which is easy but boring.

*2* Arrange for paired reading practice to take place every day for at least six weeks.

**3** Look at the book together. Discuss the title and the 'blurb' on the cover; then thumb through the pages, pointing out the names of the main characters, looking at the pictures, and outlining the story. This aids *reading for meaning*.

**4** Now start to read the book properly. **Read a short section to the child**, whilst running your finger under the print – so that he is actually looking at each word as he hears it. (A 'short section' means somewhere between a sentence and a paragraph or two. This will depend on the age and ability of the child.)

**5** **You and the child should now read the *same* passage *aloud TOGETHER*** – perhaps he can point to the words by this stage.

**6** **Now, the child should read the *same* passage *aloud BY HIMSELF*.**

**7** If he hesitates (allow 3–4 seconds), or makes a mistake, **tell** him the word or phrase straight away, encourage him to **repeat** it, and then carry on.

**8** Continue reading in this way, section by section, discussing the content at appropriate intervals, to ensure comprehension.*

The child has now read all the words he didn't know, correctly, three times in quick succession. His sight vocabulary will gradually become larger. You will find that long/unusual words (e.g. *aeroplane, dinosaur*) are learned more quickly than small 'easy' ones that look a bit like several others (e.g. *sharp/sheep/sleep*).

**As the child becomes more confident and skilled, he may prefer to leave out stage 4, or to do *Shared Reading* with you. Here, helper and child read *alternate* passages, with the helper supporting, as in stage 7.**

### The rules

- Establish a routine – a special time and place for reading. A little each day (say ten minutes) is much better than a lot once a week.

- Be positive and patient. An encouraging atmosphere is vital, particularly if the child is anxious or frustrated about his reading.

- **Show** that you are pleased with the child for trying to read. **Praise** whatever aspects of his reading behaviour you can – for example, reading with expression, getting *lots* right, reading long or difficult words, intelligent guesses, being interested in the story, not wriggling; or whatever!

- Keep a record of time spent reading and reward (merit points, stickers, etc.) for each ten minutes or whatever is appropriate for the child. The child's class teacher will probably have provided a reading record book already, so the efforts made at home can be acknowledged at school too.

- **Never** imply that a child could do better, either by word or facial expression (watch your eyebrows!). Do **not** tell him to '*Sound it out*', '*Break it up*'; '*Look at it again*', or '*Think carefully*', or point out that he knows a word because he read it on the page before. **Just quietly tell him what the word is, time**

---

* If comprehension is a particular issue, encourage the child to summarise what happened at regular intervals and say what he thinks might happen *next*. Link the story with his own personal experience, where possible.

**and time again, for as long as necessary.** Total reassurance and support is the order of the day.

■ **Keep** up the momentum of **daily** practice for at least the first six weeks. Remember that poor readers read far *less* than good readers and so do not gain even an 'average' amount of exposure to print. The Matthew Effect – 'The rich get richer and the poor get poorer' – is often quoted in this context!

## Personnel for paired reading

The person 'pair-reading' with a child must be trained to adhere to the method and have the ability to remain calm, positive and encouraging at all times. He/she must also have the time to read with the child every day. Clearly, the person best placed to do this is a parent or other family member.

In school, parent volunteers, teaching assistants and older pupils can also train in paired reading techniques. The child can also pair-read with a taped or CD-ROM version of a book, or act as helper to a younger child (very good for self-esteem!).

*Note:* You need to emphasise, if you are training parents/carers to do paired reading as described above, that it should *not* replace the bed-time story for young children. Modelling reading for relaxation and pleasure is important. Research suggests that it is particularly encouraging for boys, if their fathers read to them regularly.

---

**Useful reference:**
The website 'Interventions for Literacy, what really works for children with literacy difficulties', at www.interventionsforliteracy.org.uk, is intended to help you weigh up the choices between different published schemes and methods. The information it contains was updated, following recommendations of the Rose Report (2009), by Prof Greg Brooks: 'The only schemes included are those which are readily available and have been quantitatively evaluated in the UK, and for which at least one reasonable impact measure has been calculated, where *reasonable* implies that the scheme has been shown in at least one study to double pupils' normal rate of progress.'

## Key points for teaching reading

This handbook is not intended to be a teaching manual. However, some general principles apply which should be useful in helping SENCOs and others to put in place some teaching strategies which address the learning needs identified.

■ Children must be supported to learn to read, using as many strategies and approaches as necessary.

■ Books must be appealing, meaningful and age-appropriate.

■ Readers' interests and preferences must be taken into account.

■ Grapheme–phoneme correspondences must be established using clear instruction, producing pure sounds (so *mmm* not *muh*), and using objects or pictures which accurately represent the grapheme being taught (so insect for short/i/, not ice-cream!)

■ Phonics teaching should be multi-sensory, accurate, lively and interesting and include plenty of repetition.

■ After the delivery of systematic phonic teaching, and allowing ample time for over-learning and consolidation, staff should have the confidence to move away from phonics, when it does not appear to be working, and concentrate on other strategies which support reading development.

■ Children who are struggling with their reading should be heard reading aloud *individually* on a daily basis, for a sustained period of time, both at school and at home.

■ There is a direct correlation between undertaking regular reading practice and becoming a fluent reader.

■ A sight vocabulary of high-frequency and personal words should be taught using multi-sensory techniques, mnemonics and whatever memorable techniques will assist the pupil.

■ Paired reading should be undertaken, with adequate training beforehand (use Figure 5.1 as a handout).

# 6  Writing

'Even when good progress has been made within reading, problems with spelling and writing may persist as part of continuing difficulties in encoding, i.e. turning sounds into print... there is no doubt that problems with spelling and writing are an enduring characteristic of dyslexia.'

Rose Report (2009)

However, some children have difficulties related to the *physical* aspects of handwriting, which are often in addition to dyslexic difficulties and make it hard for them to demonstrate what they know in any legible way. This means that their speed of writing can be painfully slow and by the time they have got their first sentence down on paper, they have forgotten subsequent points.

# What you need to know

The specific learning difficulty which may be at the root of **handwriting** problems is **Developmental Coordination Disorder (DCD)**, more commonly known as *dyspraxia*. Children with such difficulties are prey to a wide range of problems affecting their educational progress as well as their organisational and social skills, their leisure pursuits and self-esteem. It is hard for them to shine on the sports field, join in a game of football in the playground, or even ride a bike, which might compensate for their frustrations in the classroom.

DCD is clearly a crucial issue in relation to handwriting and – indirectly – spelling, since one important route to learning, motor patterning, is likely to be impaired. Therefore Key Stage 1 staff should be as alert to the possibility of problems with fine motor skills as they should be to language difficulties, since the sooner help is instituted the less likely there is to be a long-term problem.

It is worth pointing out that Specific Learning Difficulties of different types (e.g. dyslexia, dyspraxia) often co-occur and you may observe features of both in the same child.

Some basic writing problems will be amenable to focused, specific teaching, while others will be intractable and require a totally different approach.

**Handwriting** is extremely difficult to alter or improve beyond Key Stage 1 and it is hugely important to establish good habits *as early as possible*. Certainly up to the end of Key Stage 1, children should be taught how to hold the pencil conventionally, form letters correctly, develop legible, cursive writing skills, construct meaningful sentences and accurately **spell** a substantial body of commonly occurring words.

In Key Stage 2 and beyond, the skilled professional must have the confidence to know when tried and tested techniques for teaching spelling have been exhausted, because some children with dyslexic-type difficulties will rarely be able to reproduce all the spelling patterns they need in independent free writing – which is, after all, the ultimate goal.

Sadly, for too many secondary school pupils, focused spelling teaching still consists of copying out lists of words, either in word families or from previously collected, random spelling errors which pupils are encouraged to commit to memory. The test of the effectiveness of such efforts is whether pupils can reproduce the words accurately when they need them in their writing. If they can't, then this enormous concentration on spelling has been futile and the time would have been better spent on other aspects of writing, as discussed below.

We have seen in Chapters 3 and 4 that blending and segmenting are reversible processes: we use them for both reading (decoding) and spelling (encoding). When we look at a printed word and break it up, we need to blend the sounds together in order to read it. When spelling, we segment (sound out) the target word orally, before trying to write it. Children should be able to make use of these reversible processes in tackling what they want to write.

When we think about writing skills, we should be very clear that this encompasses the two important aspects of writing – namely the compositional and transcriptional aspects.

**Compositional** aspects relate to the message, the content, the information contained therein and the structure. **Transcriptional** aspects, often referred to as the 'surface features' of writing, include spelling, punctuation and grammar. Handwriting would also come under the 'transcriptional' heading.

Both dimensions of writing are equally important for teaching purposes, but ultimately it is the message that matters the most.

# Practical assessment

## Free writing

A piece of unaided, uncorrected free writing is probably the first item a specialist teacher (a teacher with a postgraduate qualification in the assessment and teaching of pupils with specific learning difficulties) would ask to see, as it will reveal, almost at a glance, what a pupil's main difficulties are. Using specific tests enables a more in-depth consideration of one issue at a time:

■ Is the pupil's **handwriting** reasonably legible and tidy when he has to write at length?

■ If not, a closer inspection as suggested below may be warranted.

**Spelling** should always be looked at in free writing, as well as through administration of a test. This is because pupils whose spelling is not yet very secure cannot maintain the same standard attained in a formal test, when they are focused on other issues such as content and presentation. Are the relative proportions of phonetic, non-phonetic and bizarre examples (as described on page 75) similar, or does the balance change at all when the pupil is busy trying to think what to say or trying to keep his handwriting neat?

Look at the **content** in terms of length, organisation and grammar:

- Does the pupil write an adequate amount compared to his peers?
- Is there a beginning, middle and end, with a clear progression from one section to the next?
- Has he demarcated sections into paragraphs appropriately?
- Is the vocabulary at the expected level for his age?
- Is his grammar acceptable both at word and sentence level (see Chapter 2)?
- Is his use of punctuation appropriate for his age?

Note your main observations on the **Free writing checklist** (Figure 6.1) and consider what the pupil's most urgent needs are, in terms of in-depth assessment and learning support.

## Handwriting and motor skills

In addition to the informal observation and careful profiling of motor skills incumbent on Early Years practitioners, there is a fully standardised checklist available:

### The Movement Assessment Battery for Children Checklist, 2nd edition
(Henderson, S. & Sugden, D., 2007, Pearson)

**Age range:** 5–12 years

Through observation over at least a month, by adults in regular contact with the child, a range of observations about self-care, classroom, PE and recreational skills are made. These are considered in static/predictable environments (using a pencil to write) and dynamic/unpredictable settings (ball games). In each case the observer must rate whether the child can carry out the action *Very well, Just OK, Almost* or *Not close*. A third section asks questions about non-motor factors that can affect movement, such as timidity or impulsivity. A simple traffic light system of scoring helps the SENCO to decide whether some intervention or a referral to an educational psychologist, paediatrician, paediatric occupational therapist or physiotherapist is indicated.

## Informal assessment of handwriting

The key issues which should be closely monitored in the Early Years are:

### Posture
- Does the pupil sit up straight, feet on the floor, with the paper directly in front of him, whilst holding it steady with his non-writing hand?

# FREE WRITING CHECKLIST

**Pupil's name:**                                **Age:**

**Assessed by:**                               **Date:**

| Key issues | Observations |
|---|---|
| Handwriting/ legibility | |
| Spelling: main types of error | |
| Content relevant and appropriate? | |
| Quantity | |
| Organisation and development | |
| Vocabulary | |
| Grammar | |
| Punctuation | |

**Figure 6.1**      Special Needs Language & Literacy Assessment Handbook: photocopy master

- ■ … or is he sprawling all over the table, holding his head with one hand while the paper or exercise book slides around?

## Grip

- ■ Is the ideal tripod grip on the pencil established?
- ■ Does he consistently use the same hand to write?
- ■ Is he right- or left-handed?

## Paper

- ■ Does the pupil normally write on lined paper?
- ■ Are the lines appropriately spaced for the pupil?

## Letter formation

- ■ Does he form all his **letters** correctly?
- ■ Are the midzone letters (the round bits) all much the same size?
- ■ Are the ascenders and descenders of an appropriate length and all sloping in the same direction?
- ■ If he is 'joining up', are the horizontal and diagonal **joins** all secure?
- ■ Is he able to keep all the letters 'sitting' on the line, or do they rise up and dip below?
- ■ Are there even and appropriate sized spaces between letters and words?
- ■ Does he use capital letters and full stops correctly?
- ■ Does the older pupil use paragraphs appropriately?
- ■  Does he complain that his hand or arm aches when he has to write for any length of time?

Using the **Handwriting Checklist** (Figure 6.2), make notes in the *Observations* column about which issues need addressing. Decide on the priority needs and choose the *first* to be worked on with the pupil and transfer it to his IEP.

# Formal assessment of handwriting

The only fully standardised handwriting test on the market currently is not normed below the age of nine years. It becomes a useful tool for the SENCO concerned about children approaching the end of Key Stage 2 and secondary transfer.

## Detailed Assessment of Handwriting (DASH)
(Barnett, A., Henderson, S., Scheib, B. & Schultz, J., 2007, Pearson)

**Age range:** 9–16 years 11 months

**Time taken:** 30 minutes maximum

# HANDWRITING CHECKLIST

**Pupil's name:**                                      **Age:**

**Assessed by:**                                   **Date:**

| Key issues | Observations |
|---|---|
| Posture, position of paper and non-writing hand | |
| Pencil grip<br>Handedness – L or R? | |
| Lined/unlined paper | |
| Letter formation | |
| Size of midzone letters | |
| Height of ascenders and length of descenders | |
| Uniform slope of ascenders/descenders? | |
| Horizontal/diagonal joins | |
| Do all letters/words 'sit' on the line? | |
| Are letters and words evenly spaced? | |
| Capitals and full stops | |
| Use of paragraphs | |
| Relaxed or tense when writing?<br>Complains that hand/arm aches? | |

**Figure 6.2**     Special Needs Language & Literacy Assessment Handbook: photocopy master

This test focuses on the *mechanics* of handwriting by means of separate subtests which break the process down into fine motor skills, letter formation, sentence writing and free writing. Each subtest is strictly timed and clear marking criteria are provided. When copying out the test sentence, pupils must complete the task twice – once in their best writing and then as fast as they can.

The free writing task is supported by a spidergram of ideas plus time to plan, so as to keep the task as simple from the compositional perspective as possible. However, it still provides an opportunity for you to assess fluency when the pupil is thinking about spelling, punctuation and content.

*Note:* During the development of the test it was found that free writing speed varies hugely according to the subject matter and so it is *not* valid to let a student choose what he wants to write about for ten minutes and then use the test norms in the **DASH** manual. This is a fully standardised test and you must stick to the prescribed task in the manner outlined.

The standardised score for free writing speed offers an instant snapshot of how easy or difficult it is for the pupil to write at an average speed for his age. But if he cannot, the question is '*Why?*' Is it because he cannot think what to say – even on this unchallenging task? Or is he inhibited by word finding or spelling problems? Does he have a motor skills problem? The profile of standardised scores on the other subtests should reveal some of the answers.

- Are his graphic (fine motor) skills poor? In this case, he will probably continue to have trouble with handwriting skills and will benefit hugely from developing effective keyboard skills and being allowed to use a word-processor/computer as much as possible, or on a permanent basis.

- Is his letter formation (on the alphabet writing test) poor – even when trying his best to be neat?

- From his performance on the sentence writing tasks, is it clear that he does not know how to 'join up', or reverts to printing when he has to speed up?

Visual inspection of all this evidence will enable you to assess where particular problems lie and set targets for remedial support. The manual contains some case studies and a brief introduction, in chapter 4, to the key issues involved in handwriting assessment.

The **DASH** can be administered to individuals or groups of pupils causing concern. The free writing task could be used for initial screening purposes and the rest of the subtests used to probe for possible problems in the group falling in the below-average range.

# Key points about handwriting

It should be noted that changing handwriting is very difficult and should be addressed as early in a pupil's school career as possible. Tackle one issue at a time and provide plenty of reinforcement activities on a daily basis. Do not expect the pupil to start work on the next target until the first is secured. You can check this yourself by inspecting his everyday work.

Ergonomic pens/pencils such as the *Penagain Twist and Write* pencil at Key Stage 1 or a *Yoropen* at Key Stage 2/3 can be very helpful, as well as the usual array of pencil grips.

A little time spent formatting lined writing paper which can be quickly photocopied to suit different sizes of handwriting, is of great help to Key Stage 1 pupils struggling with sizing issues.

All pupils struggling with handwriting will need extra time to produce written work, or should be required to write less than their peers, or given permission for parents to scribe part of their homework. On suitable occasions, pupils may gain much from preparing a talk rather than writing about something.

In extreme cases of handwriting difficulties, an amanuensis (scribe) during exams may be required. Good keyboard skills and access to a computer will be the key to success in the long run, for pupils whose handwriting difficulties are intransigent.

# Spelling

When choosing a spelling test, or evaluating the one you currently use, look carefully at the date it was standardised. If you want accurate spelling test results, only use one that was standardised recently, such as:

**Graded Word Spelling Test,** 3rd edition
(Vernon, P.E., revised and restandardised by McCarty & Crumpler, 2006, Hodder Education)

**Age range:** 5–18 years

This long established test, recently restandardised, contains eighty words graded in increasing order of difficulty. Table 1 in the manual shows which section is likely to be most suitable for each age group – although there is no bar to starting and/or stopping at an easier (or harder) point if this is thought appropriate. When testing individuals the process is likely to be quicker, as after starting at the point appropriate to the testee's age, each fifth word is offered until he starts to make mistakes (see page 6) and then stopped when he has made a total of ten errors. In this way, the discretion and judgment of the teacher helps to cut down the time taken on the test.

The words to be spelled are dictated in a sentence (set out in the manual) so that the pupil should not get caught out by homophones of the *been/bean* variety. Pupils are allowed about fifteen seconds to respond to each item, and are not allowed rubbers – they must cross out attempts with which they are unhappy and rewrite them. This enables the marker to see when several attempts are made, although when assessing on a one-to-one basis this can be directly observed. A simple scoring system provides the raw data to look up the standardised score and also percentiles and Spelling Age if preferred.

It is possible to carry out a simple **error analysis**, marking up the errors as *ph* for good phonetic representations, even if not quite the right spelling (*sed* for *said*; *kik* for *kick*, *pashents* for *patience*, etc.); *syll* for longer words where one or more syllables are **not** represented (*remebr* for *remember*, *beging* for *beginning*), and *biz* for bizarre (e.g. *sgr* for *grass*). Total the three types up and you will have an immediate picture of the pupil's main needs in terms of learning support. For more information, see Chapter 7.

## Spelling error analysis

Support for spelling is dependent on age, stage and pressing need.

If a **five year old** writes *'wunsaponatim'* for *'once upon a time'*, this is not a spelling error, but is an example of developmental (alphabetic) spelling. In this case the child is displaying the very secure ability to use phonetic spelling (writing what you hear). What this child needs to develop next is an understanding of word boundaries: where one word ends and the next one begins. You can detect too, in this example, a confusion between the letter name *I* and split digraph *i–e*. But this is also developmental spelling and should not give cause for concern.

If a **six year old** writer uses the graphemes *chrayn* to represent *train*, again this is developmental and should resolve once he learns the correct pronunciation or makes the link with the word *train* in his reading books**.** The teacher might monitor a child's pronunciation, using a mirror to look at the positioning of lips, tongue and teeth.

Up to the end of Key Stage 1, if a child writes *raddit* for *rabbit*, then letter sound confusion is present (*b/d*). This can easily be addressed by multi-sensory teaching using mnemonics or personally significant triggers. For example, if his brother is called Bob, start with the /b/ because once you have established *one* of the confusable graphemes, you will have a firm starting point on which to build. The main thing with letter shapes which can easily be confused – like *b*, *d* and *p* – is to *'keep trouble apart'* (Brand, 1984) and teach them separately, with a good interval between them.

There is a world of difference between plausible phonetic spelling alternatives and truly bizarre spelling. So if on examination of a child's free writing you encounter errors which cannot be mediated by intelligent guesswork or prior knowledge, and the child himself cannot tell you what he intended to write, then you need to refer him to a specialist teacher for urgent, in-depth, diagnostic assessment. The type of spelling which would be categorised as bizarre might be something on the lines of *'SeI cjikg mi drepliz fr Mm.'*

# 7 Common Spelling and Writing Problems . . . and some solutions

## Problem 1: Common letter strings not known
## Solution: Spelling by analogy (onset and rime)

If a particular letter string is giving difficulty – e.g. *'dreeming'* for *dreaming* – then onset and rime work on /ea/ will be helpful. This can be done through focused practice on the *–eam* chunk, with different initial phonemes and consonant clusters – also known as **onset and rime**. An example, where you could use colour to highlight the rime chunk, is:

> t–*eam*
>
> b–*eam*
>
> cr–*eam*
>
> dr–*eam*
>
> st–*eam*
>
> str–*eam*

Teaching through onset and rime groupings means that the child is working with larger chunks of sound than single phonemes. This reduces the load on 'working memory' and is likely to be much more effective than the blending and segmenting of single phonemes if the pupil has phonological processing difficulties.

- Always start with the most frequently occurring patterns first.
- Provide plenty of opportunity for over-learning and reinforcement.
- Always use the words *in sentences*, to reinforce the essential link between both spelling patterns and meaning. Spelling patterns are often dependent on meaning in context (e.g. *been/bean*).
- Encourage use of colour to highlight the pattern being worked on,
- Writing the words out on coloured card – using rainbow pencils, glitter pens or whatever appeals – will be of help, as long as auditory feedback is provided by the pupil saying aloud what he is writing.
- It is well known that the power of your 'own voice' is the most potent learning tool.

Note that onset and rime work will also assist with specific reading problems, such as reading *dream* as *drim,* or *team* as *te–am.*

## Problem 2: Weak knowledge of high-frequency/key words
## Solution: Look, Say, Cover, Write and Check (LSCWC)

For key words which have to be committed to memory, we recommend ***Look, Say, Cover, Write and Check*** (LSCWC). Taught properly, this will work, but it is important that this exercise does not become merely 'copying out'. For LCSWC to be really effective, the child has to say the *letter sounds or names* (whichever works best) whilst writing and must cover up the target word before attempting it. It then needs to be checked and correctly repeated at least ten times. This is truly multi-sensory, since it is reinforcing motor memory by the writing and rewriting of the whole word and provides auditory feedback, using one's own voice.

## Problem 3: Omission of syllables
## Solution: Syllabification

Where a child telescopes or foreshortens words such as *rember* for *remember* or *beging* for *beginning,* the solution is to teach the basics of **syllabification**. This can be taught by encouraging the pupil to tap/beat out each syllable he hears.

In English each syllable must contain at least one vowel and this includes **–y** in words like *dry* or *happy*. So by using children's names, this fun activity can be harnessed to teach the rudiments of syllabification:

> Sam = 1 syllable
>
> Pe/ter = 2 syllables
>
> O/li/ver = 3 syllables
>
> Ha/rry = 2 syllables
>
> A/lex/an/der = 4 syllables

Teaching syllabification is easy and interactive using clapping, tapping with a makeshift hammer or using *chin bumps,* where the back of the hand is placed under the chin and as each syllable is pronounced there is a downward pressure felt on the hand.

## Problem 4: Common word endings not known
## Solution: Teach suffixes

This is an area of spelling where children can make progress quickly and easily. It relates to common endings (suffixes) and morphemes.

A **morpheme** is the smallest unit of language which carries meaning. So /s/ is a morpheme which denotes the plural in *dogs. Dog* itself is a morpheme because it represents the concept of a dog and /s/ is a morpheme because it tells us that there is more than one dog. So knowing how to make plurals is very productive.

In this context, knowing about the 'bound' morphemes like *–ing* and *–ed* will also be helpful in eradicating errors like *walkt (walked), wantid (wanted)* and *playng (playing).*

## Problem 5: Confuses s/c and j/g
## Solution: Teach soft and hard /c/ and /g/ spelling rule

Once children grasp how the hard and soft /g/ and /c/ work, this can eradicate a whole raft of errors. All they really need to know is that when used before *a, o* or *u* the /c/ and /g/ are hard (*cat, cot, cut; gap, got, gut*) and when used before /e/, /i/ or /y/ they are usually soft (*cent, circle, cycle, gem, giant, gym*). Once you have heard a pupil read *city centre* as *kitty kentree*, you realise the usefulness of this particular rule!

## Problem 6: Content irrelevant or inappropriate to the task set; poorly organised
## Solution: Provide planning and structuring formats

For the pupil who finds planning and organising his ideas into paragraphs really difficult, the Hickey Six Frame (Hickey, 1977) is a useful tool, in addition to spidergrams, writing frames and mind-maps.

### Hickey Six Frame
Pupils are given six frames of an appropriate size for their age and asked to draw a picture and write a sentence or a whole paragraph (according to age and ability) in each one. The headings are:

1. The people.
2. The place.
3. Something begins to happen.
4. The exciting bit.
5. It all gets sorted out.
6. Tie up loose ends.

For example:

| 1. The people | 2. The place | 3. Something begins to happen |
|---|---|---|
| Gill and Prue went out for a walk. | They went to the woods with the dog. | Gill tripped over a big log. |
| **4. The exciting bit** | **5. It all gets sorted out** | **6. Tie up loose ends** |
| Underneath it she saw some shiny keys. | They took the keys to the police station. | The man who lost them was very pleased to get them back. |

This method teaches pupils to balance their writing and not write *so* much at the beginning that they have no time or space to finish.

# Should the focus of learning support change during Key Stage 2?

It is difficult to be prescriptive about *when* the main focus of learning support should shift from focusing almost exclusively on spellings to teaching **study skills**. In our opinion, this would generally apply by the end of Key Stage 2. If all a pupil's spelling errors are good phonetic attempts, he is well on the way to being able to communicate in writing effectively.

- As he progresses through Key Stage 2 he needs to learn to use a high-frequency word bank, cue cards, and a small *spelling* **dictionary**. Many children are only provided with and taught to use conventional dictionaries, which tend to be rather dense.

- Poor spellers will benefit from being taught to use the simpler and shorter spelling dictionaries (e.g. *Spell it Yourself*, Hawker, G.T., 1981, Oxford University Press). If a pupil wants to use a word when writing, he probably already knows what it means!

- Many pupils will benefit from learning to use an **electronic** *phonetic* **spell-checker/dictionary** (e.g. Franklin machines), which works on the same principle as the spellchecker in Microsoft Word and thus provides an excellent grounding for future IT skills. Technology and gadgets are seen to be cool!

- It is worth noting that in public exams such as GCSEs the percentage of marks for SPAG (spelling, punctuation and grammar) is relatively small and will make little difference to the overall grade. So provided the writing can be interpreted – e.g. *Nepollian* for *Napoleon* – it is more important to concentrate on structuring the answer appropriately, and responding to the question set, than getting sidetracked by issues of spelling accuracy.

# Marking policy

Teachers are much more likely to comment on the **surface** features of a pupil's writing than the content, for obvious reasons: it is much quicker and easier to mark spelling errors, to comment on misplaced capital letters and full stops, and to let a child know you can't decipher his writing, than to provide thoughtful analysis about the content.

However, for children who struggle with writing, it is much more important to comment on the **content** of their work: as long as this content is accessible to the reader, we should focus on that rather than the surface features. We need to comment on content, using as much positive language as possible.

One useful technique is the '*3 stars and a wish*' approach, which requires teachers to say three good things about a child's writing and identify one specific area for improvement. For example:

### 3 stars

★ You do know a lot about dinosaurs, Gracie.

★ I like the way your story had an exciting ending.

★ I was very glad to know you all got home from the museum safely.

### and a wish

🖉 In your next story, please try to remember to use full stops at the end of every sentence.

---

## Key points for supporting writing

■ Deal with one aspect of writing at a time, since it is hard for the pupil to concentrate on content *and* spelling/punctuation/handwriting together.

■ Investigate writing materials, to ensure the best pen/pencil grip and paper.

■ Teach dictionary and study skills.

■ When supporting spelling, focus only on high-frequency words which must be committed to memory, so teach *friend* but not *freckle*.

■ Provide writing frames and formats to aid composition.

■ Use technology as a helpful adjunct, e.g. word processing and electronic spellcheckers.

■ Evaluate the quantity of writing required. If this is problematical, consider asking a teaching assistant to scribe at school and parents/carers at home.

■ Provide positive feedback and comments which support the development of *content* rather than over-emphasising the spelling, grammar and punctuation.

# 8    The Secondary School

*By **Hannah Williams**, in conjunction with colleagues from the London Borough of Newham Learning Support Service, SpLD Team*

If you are reading this chapter you are probably responsible for helping to support pupils whose literacy skills are currently inadequate for their needs. Secondary schools are notoriously difficult places in which to support these pupils, due to their size and structure.

This chapter aims to support a secondary SENCO with limited experience of Specific Literacy Difficulties (SpLD). It offers advice on choosing suitable assessments and setting up successful interventions, which must then be effectively monitored and progress recorded accurately. It will also offer simple but effective ways to support colleagues teaching learners with literacy difficulties.

By the time pupils reach Year 7, it is more difficult for them to make progress than at primary school if they are still struggling to read and write – but not impossible. Students with the most severe difficulties can still acquire new skills if taught with the right intensity (Torgeson, 2007).

Secondary school learning is largely focused on text-based activities and written communication, which can create barriers to learning. If pupils cannot access text efficiently they will experience comprehension difficulties – and language comprehension difficulties at this age can themselves often be overlooked. If pupils have difficulties reading, it is generally put down to their poor decoding skills or the fact that they have a very limited sight vocabulary. To be a fluent reader one needs to have both adequate decoding *and* language comprehension skills (see Chapters 2, 3 and 4).

The Rose Review (2009), referred to in previous chapters, cannot be too highly recommended as a resource rich in excellent, practical advice for secondary teachers. The report states that secondary pupils with persistent reading difficulties are in danger of developing entrenched negative attitudes, a feeling of disaffection and disengagement. Therefore getting the support right for them is imperative.

# A model for support and intervention

If you are responsible for improving current practice in your school setting, then you are an 'agent of change'. To ensure success, make sure your approach includes time for everyone involved to assimilate and implement new ideas.

As SENCO you might view your school as a machine in which the component parts work together purposefully to produce the desired outcome. This machine needs to be considered on two levels:

*1*  A **macro level**, where you consider the implications for staff, ensuring a consistent approach to dyslexia and literacy difficulties in your school, and helping to create an ethos in which all staff have a role to play, which is supported by senior management and parents.

*2*  A **micro level**, where you consider individual pupils, their specific learning needs, and how best to deliver them,

The challenge for the secondary SENCO is to:

■ create and maintain a robust and effective system of identification and assessment, followed by the delivery of focused intervention. There should be a high level of consistency in the school's approach to students who may be dyslexic;

■ have a system in place which allows for the onward referral of pupils to other specialists where necessary, according to your protocols. You should be able to collect and present evidence to specialist teachers/educational psychologists to assist them in making a diagnosis. Documentary evidence collected in this way will also contribute to any applications for access arrangements during public examinations (see Chapter 9).

The following sections will support you in building this machine in an organised and transparent way.

# At the 'macro' level – management

## Policy

■ Establish a threshold to identify all pupils with literacy difficulties. At entry to secondary school, this could be National Curriculum levels* or standardised scores on reading and spelling tests, if available. Use this transition data to decide which pupils to assess; or consider screening the entire intake.

■ During Year 7, identify those pupils who require additional or more intensive intervention.

■ Gain the active support of senior management and teaching staff for the policy of withdrawing pupils for intervention.

■ If needed, adapt and amend the SEN policy and other whole-school documents to reflect change.

■ Include in your SENCO Action Plan desired outcomes for the year, for SpLD pupils, so that appropriate funding is agreed by relevant staff.

## Staff training

■ Consider the financial implications of staff training, in terms of delivery costs as well as cover for teachers and teaching assistants.

---

* It is worth reviewing the accuracy and consistency of NC levels reported by feeder primary schools.

- Schedule staff INSET to demonstrate intervention and support strategies across the curriculum. Include strategies that they can all use and adapt which will help remove barriers to learning in their specific subjects. Figure 8.1 provides a photocopiable handout of helpful strategies for Key Stages 3/4 classroom teachers.

- Create a forum for good practice to be shared, so that a resource bank of ideas between staff is created, covering initiatives such as Paired Reading (see page 62) and Study Support Groups. This will help to enable successful differentiation and good Quality First Teaching.

- Create opportunities for support staff leading intervention groups to share good practice and experiences with subject teachers.

- Keep the channels of communication open at all times and problem-solve challenges together.

- Staff who are trained to administer assessments and analyse the results properly are needed for working with individual pupils. Training should be undertaken with a specialist provider. Select staff with a genuine interest in the field of SpLD, as the outcomes will be more effective. Remember that only qualified teaching staff should be administering standardised assessments.

- Further training may be required to support successful delivery of interventions. Training time must be factored into whole-school timetables, and the financial implications considered.

## Purchasing

- Select and purchase (as necessary) appropriate assessment and support materials. Include resources – such as IT programs that can be used independently by pupils with adult guidance – to support children who are struggling with the literacy demands of the curriculum, but who may not meet the threshold to warrant a full assessment.

## Time management

- Allocate time for designated staff to analyse pupils' attainments, to identify those needing further action and decide on the interventions.

- Allocate the required resources to staff and ensure rooms are available for learning support sessions. IT-based interventions will need support from your technicians.

Learning support needs to be carried out *consistently* to have the greatest chance of success. So allocate time to undertake **reviews** of intervention as soon as you get your diary! Schedule regular meetings between teaching assistants and teachers delivering support every half-term to discuss pupil progress and next steps. Having these meetings scheduled has a dual purpose: not only does it add value to what teaching assistants or teachers are doing, because they feel someone cares about the outcomes, but it also enables you to have a clear picture of what is working and what needs adjusting.

# SUPPORT STRATEGIES

## Lesson Introduction

Give the learning objective in clear simple language together with the 'big picture' of the lesson. Show how this connects with previous learning.

Alert pupils to the sequence of activities during the lesson.

Display key words in a clearly visible position.

Use visuals and multi-sensory stimuli.

## General Strategies during the Lesson

Highlight the main points of the lesson as they occur.

Pause and sum up frequently.

Seat pupils with literacy difficulties where they can see you and easily access information.

Ensure they have time to complete tasks before moving on to the next one.

Give them individual key word lists at the beginning of every new topic.

## Copying

For pupils who cannot copy accurately from the board, provide notes as handouts in advance of the lesson.

Provide written information in large clear font – not too much text, graphics and colour-coded where necessary.

Use coloured pens on the white board to demarcate lines of information.

Print information on the white board for the pupils who have difficulties copying.

## Questions

Give pupils time to formulate responses to questions (e.g. *'In a moment I'm going to ask you all….'*).

Address some questions directly to targeted pupils, using their name(s).

Use true/false or forced alternative techniques (e.g. *Is it this or is it that?*)

## Reading

Introduce the text by referring to the title, pictures and key words, and giving a brief summary.

Ensure that texts are appropriate in terms of reading level.

Organise paired and group reading.

Produce worksheets/handouts double or one and a half spaced with a large clear font (e.g. Comic Sans/Ariel, size 16–20).

## Comprehension

Give clear, simple instructions to the class; short and varied activities.

Ask questions to check understanding of text or topic, as well as new vocabulary.

Ask pupils to repeat key information to check their understanding.

| Recording (and alternatives to traditional written recording) |
|---|
| Provide models of quality written work and appropriate dictionaries. |
| Give sentence starters, word banks and subject specific writing frames. |
| Encourage use of flowcharts, pictures, charts, mind maps, photos, etc. |
| Use techniques such as sequencing sentences, cloze procedure and/or multiple-choice tick lists for pupils with reading comprehension difficulties. |
| Allow oral presentations, scribed work and use of ICT programmes such as Clicker 5 for pupils with writing problems to demonstrate their understanding. |

| Homework |
|---|
| Write up homework tasks in the same place at the **beginning** of each lesson, and ensure all pupils write it down immediately and clearly in their homework diary or planner. |
| Make sure homework is appropriate, can be completed independently by all pupils and is related to class work. |
| Check that support is provided for homework completion (e.g. homework club, peer support). |

| Revision |
|---|
| Demonstrate study skills techniques – e.g. highlighting key words, using bullet points, taking and storing notes. |

| Use of Support Staff |
|---|
| Timetable meetings between subject and support staff for planning. |
| Ensure support staff are aware of the content of the lesson and the expected outcomes for pupils. |
| Use them flexibly – not always with the same pupils. |
| Encourage support staff to prompt pupils with questions and answers, and to follow up the main points with them. |

| Marking and Assessment |
|---|
| Ensure there is provision for all students within the school's marking and assessment policies. |
| If appropriate, mark separately for content/ideas and presentation (including spelling, punctuation and grammar). |
| Emphasise the positive by comments such as *'The things I liked about this work were …', 'It would have been better if …'*. |

Special Needs Language & Literacy Assessment Handbook: photocopy master

**Figure 8.1:** Support strategies for Key Stage 3 and 4 classroom teachers*

* Reproduced with permission from London Borough of Newham, *Literacy For All* Policy, 2009.

# At the 'micro' level – individual support

- Assess pupils individually or in groups.
- Find out what intervention programmes pupils have been working on in the past and what progress was made.
- Use the results to set up appropriate interventions.
- Establish a clear cycle of assessment–teaching–assessment for each pupil, with regular review dates specified.
- Adjust or discontinue interventions according to need.

# Practical assessment

Understanding the root of the difficulty is crucial in order to get a whole picture of the learner. It is important for those leading the intervention to discover a pupil's **strengths**, as well as his specific **needs.**

# Reading skills

A good starting point is to familiarise yourself with the 'simple view of reading' (see Chapter 4). This highlights the two most important aspects of reading: word recognition and language comprehension.

When a learner appears to be experiencing difficulties, the first step is therefore to assess his:

- single-word reading accuracy
- reading comprehension of text.

Ensuring that you have the resources to make accurate assessments is therefore important. Suggested resources are :

## Single Word Reading Test 6–16
(Foster, H., 2008, GL Assessment)

**Age range:** 6–16 years

- This oral test is quick to administer, to individual pupils.
- It has parallel forms for retesting.
- It can be used to assess eligibility for reading assistance during exams.

## Access Reading Test
(McCarty, C. & Crumpler, M., 2006, Hodder Education)

**Age range:** 7–20+

**Time allowed:** 30 minutes.

**Parallel forms?** Yes

This reading comprehension test can be used with groups as well as individual pupils. It can also be re-scored after 25% extra time has been allowed, to see if an application for extra time during examinations might be appropriate.

Interactive single-user and networkable versions are also available, and include the facility to compare assessments with and without extra time automatically.

*(for a fuller description of this test, see Chapter 4)*

## Diagnostic Reading Analysis, 2nd edition
(Crumpler, M. & McCarty, C., 2008, Hodder Education)

**Age range:** 6 years 6 months–16 years 5 months

**Time needed:** about 15 minutes.

**Parallel forms?** Yes

This orally administered individual test gives measures of listening comprehension, reading accuracy (at text level), speed of reading at text level, comprehension of text and comprehension processing speed

*(for a fuller description of this test, see Chapter 4)*

# Writing skills

You will also need to administer a spelling test and assess a sample of uncorrected, unaided free writing. Suitable spelling tests are:

## Single Word Spelling Test
(Sacre, L. & Masterson, J., 2000, GL Assessment)

**Age range:** 5–14 years

- Photocopiable record forms are available.
- There are different spellings for different ages.
- It can be used diagnostically to identify gaps in pupils' spelling knowledge.
- Pupils with difficulties can be given a test considered appropriate for their ability not their age.
- An online version is available.

## Helen Arkell Spelling Test (HAST)
Part 1 – Word Spelling Test (Helen Arkell Dyslexia Centre, 1998)

(Part 2 – Diagnostic Spelling Test currently being restandardised)

**Age range:** 5–17 years

- It is easy to administer to groups and/or single pupils.

- The words are chosen to represent the normal development of spelling.

### Graded Word Spelling Test, 3rd edition
(Vernon, P. E., McCarty, C. & Crumpler, M., 2006, Hodder Education)

**Age range:** 5 years 5 months–17 years 5 months

*(for a description of this test, see Chapter 6)*

### Free writing
Assess the National Curriculum level of the pupil's writing and gauge which aspects of writing require targeted teaching (see *Free Writing Assessment* in Chapter 6, also *Writing Speed* in Chapter 9).

# Study skills

Good study skills are a vital aspect of secondary school learning, and need to be assessed and taught. Some study skills are generic and apply across the curriculum, but others will need to be covered through individual subjects.

Figure 8.2 provides questionnaires for compiling the study skills needs of an individual pupil. All learners will benefit from working in a multi-sensory way and understanding what works best for them. So discussion and development of appropriate strategies with each pupil will be helpful.

# Avoid repetition

Lastly, find out exactly what support has been given before and what intervention programmes have been used. As Torgeson (2007) reports, it is counter-productive to repeat interventions that have been tried previously and have failed. The present authors have both encountered instances of secondary school interventions which simply repeat the drills, programmes and methods already encountered. These serve no useful purpose and simply demotivate secondary pupils even more.

# STUDY SKILLS – staff questionnaire

**Pupil's name:**                                    **Age:**

**Information gathered by:**                          **Date:**

| | |
|---|---|
| **Attendance**<br>Does the pupil:<br>■ attend school regularly or arrive late/truant?<br>■ arrive at lessons punctually, with the right books and equipment? | |
| **Attitudes**<br>Does the pupil:<br>■ seem happy in school?<br>■ stay on task in class?<br>Is there a marked difference between his/her **oral** contributions and **written** work? | |
| **Homework**<br>Does the pupil:<br>■ complete it satisfactorily?<br>■ hand it in on time?<br>Does it take him/her hours? | |
| **Tests and exams**<br>How does he/she perform?<br>■ above/below/in line with expectations for the group?<br>■ above/below/in line with expectations, given his/her apparent ability in class? | |
| Is there a marked difference between the pupil's attitude and achievements in certain subjects compared to others? | *Best*<br><br>*Worst* |

# STUDY SKILLS – pupil questionnaire

**Pupil's name:**                                          **Age:**

**Interviewer:**                                           **Date:**

| | |
|---|---|
| What is your favourite subject at school? | |
| What is your *least* favourite subject? | |
| Do you have any career or training plans? | |
| **Reading**<br><br>Do you read novels, newspapers, magazines?<br><br>How often?<br><br>How do you get on with reading for homework ? | |
| **Writing**<br><br>How do you get on with writing?<br><br>If not very well, why not?<br>*(for example, spelling, handwriting, finding the right words, or knowing what to write about)* | |
| Do you know how to plan written work and revise for tests/exams? | |
| Can you use a dictionary? | |
| Can you word-process and use the Internet? | |
| When and where do you do your homework?<br><br>Does it take you a very long time?<br><br>Does anyone help you? If so, who? | |

**Figure 8.2b**   Special Needs Language & Literacy Assessment Handbook: photocopy master

# Delivering appropriate interventions

Having identified the pupils who will need extra in-school support and those who will require more intensive intervention, amicable agreement between staff will be needed if it means pupils missing their particular subject.

The delivery of any scheme needs a high degree of consistency. Using interventions which have lesson plans already written, and a structured reading scheme, will go a long way to achieving this. Some recommended schemes are.

- *Units of Sound* (Key Stages 2, 3 and 4) – Dyslexia Action
- *Lifeboat Literacy Programme* (Key Stages 2, 3 and 4) – Robinswood Press
- *Spelling Made Easy* (Key Stages 2, 3 and 4) – www.egon.co.uk
- *Lexia* (Key Stages 1, 2, 3 and 4) – www.lexiauk.co.uk
- Phonographix programme (Key Stages 2, 3 & 4) *Reading Reflex. The foolproof Phonographix method for teaching your child to read* (1998) McGuinness, C. & McGuinness, G. – Penguin Books
- *Ready-made Lessons for Pupils with Dyslexia-type Difficulties*, by Penny Tolson (Key Stages 2, 3 and 4) – Dyslexia Action
- ReadWriteInc – www.readwriteinc.com
- *Corrective Reading* – www.mcgraw-hill.co.uk
- *Lexia Strategies for Older Readers* – www.lexiauk.co.uk
- *Successmaker* – www.rm.com

(From Wave 3/Individualised Literacy Programmes, London Borough of Newham *Literacy For All Policy*, 2009.)

The website 'Interventions for Literacy, what really works for children with literacy difficulties', at www.interventionsforliteracy.org.uk, is intended to help you weigh up the choices between different published schemes and methods. The information it contains was updated, following recommendations of the Rose Report (2009), by Prof Greg Brooks: 'The only schemes included are those which are readily available and have been quantitatively evaluated in the UK, and for which at least one reasonable impact measure has been calculated, where *reasonable* implies that the scheme has been shown in at least one study to double pupils' normal rate of progress.'

Support may need to include work on phonics and phonological awareness, but – more importantly – should include regular opportunities to read, so that pupils can extend their sight vocabulary, fluency and comprehension.

## Reading support

**Paired Reading** with peer tutors is a most effective technique to encourage reading development, and there is no cost involved in setting it up (for detailed information on how to implement paired reading, see Chapter 4). Many schools use older pupils working alongside younger pupils, and both tutor and tutee can benefit – tutors can gain credit for the Duke of Edinburgh's community service badge, for example.

There are many reading schemes on the market, but for secondary-age pupils it can be quite difficult to find books with a low reading age, but a high level of interest. Secondary-age pupils do not want to feel patronised, so build on their interests wherever possible. Encourage them to bring in their own books, magazines or comics. Use the paired reading technique to read with them, so difficult words can be accessed and fluency maintained.

The following publishers produce books suitable for secondary-age pupils in terms of content and interest levels, but which have lower reading ages (from London Borough of Newham *Literacy For All* Policy, 2009):

- Nelson Thornes – www.nelsonthornes.com
- Barrington Stoke – www.barringtonstoke.co.uk
- Hodder Education – www.hoddereducation.co.uk
- Franklin Watts – www.franklinwatts.co.uk
- Gardener Education – www.gardener-education.com
- Badger Publishing – www.badger-publishing.co.uk
- Ransom Publishing– www.ransom.co.uk
- Folens – www.folens.com
- LDA – www.LDAlearning.com
- Heinemann – www.heinemann.co.uk

## Self-esteem

Burton (2004) reported that setting up self-esteem groups for pupils resulted in a positive shift in both attitudes and literacy skills. Giving pupils allocated time to meet others with the same difficulties made them feel better about their own problems, and more able to manage the difficulties they experienced. The secondary SENCO might consider setting up such groups as part of the support package. In connection with this, setting SMART – specific, measurable, attainable, relevant and time-limited – targets which are achievable and realistic will be crucial.

## Monitoring

It is the SENCO's role to monitor interventions. Delivering an intervention programme yourself will support your understanding of what is required to ensure that pupils make progress. This input could also be used to model the process to other members of staff who might continue to deliver support.

# Finally ...

Hopefully, the above suggestions will assist your decision-making process and guide you and your school in supporting pupils to make progress. Remember to check your local authority's policies concerning assessment and interventions. If you are interested in reading the *Literacy for All* (2009) policy from which this chapter is drawn, you can purchase it from the Learning Support Service in the London Borough of Newham. It is available on DVD or as a ring-bound file.

## Key points

■ Make interventions specific to the needs of the pupils – spend time analysing the results and understanding their implications. It will be worth it.

■ Do not repeat interventions which have not worked in the past – avoid boredom!

■ The most important thing is that pupils make progress and remember what they are learning – whatever way is easiest for them!

■ Get a team around you and support the staff.

■ Link up with other secondary schools in the area to see if you can share resources, ideas and good practice.

■ Interventions need to run for a minimum of two terms. Remember to review progress at regular intervals.

■ Be creative when choosing reading materials, the important thing is to capture and maintain pupils' interest levels.

# 9 Access Arrangements in Tests and Examinations

It is essential to understand the nature and purpose of 'access arrangements' before discussing why and how a pupil might be eligible for them during any tests or examinations.

They are a means of enabling a pupil to demonstrate what he knows and can do in any formal assessment situation, if he has a learning difficulty or disability which puts him at a significant disadvantage compared to his peers or if the examination would be inaccessible to him without some adjustment. So the severely dyslexic or dyspraxic pupil with great difficulties writing fluently would be eligible for an adjustment to the exam situation (see below for some examples). The blind candidate would be entitled to Brailled question papers, and the very poor reader might need the questions read out to him.

## What you need to know

Before considering access arrangements, staff first need to be confident that it is indeed appropriate for that pupil to be entered for a test or examination – that he has sufficient knowledge to obtain a grade in the subject being assessed. During Key Stage 2 tests, it may be inappropriate for a pupil to sit the tests even though he is working at the level of the test, because (for example) he is going through a severe emotional crisis.

Once **appropriate entry** has been established, the type of adjustment to the examination conditions can be considered. This will depend on:

- the nature and severity of his difficulties: these may need to be quantified by use of standardised tests; and
- the nature of support he has been used to in school.

Access arrangements should always reflect the history of provision and the pupil's **normal way of working**. So, for example …

- If a candidate's writing difficulties are very severe and he is used to a TA scribing for him in class, or he has learned to use Dragon Naturally Speaking, say, or ViaVoice competently, then the most appropriate access arrangement would be provision of an **amanuensis** (scribe) or his usual voice-activated **word processor**.
- If, following a formal diagnostic assessment in Year 7 or 8, he has been using a laptop **in class** because of his learning difficulties (i.e. not just for completing homework), then he should be allowed to use a computer during the GCSE examinations.
- If he is an exceptionally slow reader, or normally handwrites his work, but very slowly, then he might qualify for **extra time**.
- If he is an EAL candidate, he may, under certain circumstances, be allowed to use a **bilingual dictionary**.

- If he writes quite quickly and fluently but it is really difficult for anyone else to read his script, the most appropriate arrangement might be for the TA or teacher who is familiar with his handwriting to provide a **transcript** or simply to photocopy and enlarge his answer sheet and then write the intended words clearly in red above those that are illegible.

- The student with severe attentional problems may be used to and need somebody to **'prompt'** him to stay on task, or, if the attention deficit is combined with acute hyperactivity, need an accompanied **break** half-way through the exam.

These examples give an idea of the range of possible adjustments to an assessment situation, but the complete range of possible access arrangements is outlined in the relevant regulations specified below. However, two things need to be made very clear.

**Firstly,** access arrangements should never be granted to a candidate on the grounds of learning difficulties *unless* his ability to read, write or stay on task is significantly impaired and proved by use of standardised tests during the relevant phase of education. Therefore …

- It is not permissible to give a GCSE or A level candidate extra time because he had a diagnosis of dyslexia at some time in the past if he can now read and write as well as his peers, *unless* an educational psychologist or specialist teacher (a teacher with a postgraduate qualification in the assessment and teaching of pupils with specific learning difficulties) confirms that he is still disadvantaged by a significant cognitive processing difficulty.

- Nor should a candidate use a computer during the exams because he prefers to, or uses one for all his coursework, or types faster than he can handwrite, *unless* he has significant and verifiable handwriting difficulties. Until very recently, the JCQ's view was that unless every candidate in the land is using a computer to complete all public examinations, this would be giving that candidate a very significant *unfair advantage*. However, presumably in recognition of the fact that in some schools word processors are provided for all students and it would be unfair to make those students handwrite their exams, the regulations now state that *'If a word processor is the candidate's normal way of working within the centre, then it must be used in examinations.'*

**Secondly,** the assessment objectives of national tests and public examinations are the same for everyone – a candidate cannot be given credit for a skill or knowledge which he is unable to demonstrate. So, for example, a quadriplegic candidate cannot be credited with the practical skills of carrying out scientific experiments, even though his theoretical knowledge might be very good.

# National Curriculum Tests and access arrangements in the primary school

The task of managing access arrangements during the Key Stage 2 'SATs' is much easier for primary school staff than for their colleagues in secondary schools during the run up to GCSE. By Year 6 the children requiring access arrangements should easily have been identified, because class teachers get to know their pupils well in the smaller infant and junior schools.

The primary source of information for this sector is to be found in the *Key Stage 2 Access Arrangements Guide* **(AAG),** published by:

Qualifications and Curriculum Development Agency
53–55 Butts Road,
Earlsdon Park,
Coventry
CV1 3BH

The Guide is available online in pdf format at www.qcda.gov.uk

There is no alternative to studying the regulations each year and making sure you fully understand and adhere to them. Some essential key points are as follows:

- Access arrangements should reflect the nature of support the pupil receives as part of normal classroom practice. Schools must keep the evidence demonstrating a pupil's eligibility for access arrangements on file and available for inspection.

- The range of possible access arrangements includes extra time, readers, scribes, transcripts, word processors, Brailled or enlarged print papers, prompters, and rest breaks.

- On the whole, primary school staff can make their own decisions regarding suitable support for children who have difficulties – so long as this is in keeping with normal practice. But unless a child is statemented, permission must (at the time of writing) be sought to give them extra time.

When applying for permission to provide **additional time** during Key Stage 2 tests, you will need to use up-to-date standardised reading tests to provide the necessary *evidence of need*. The resources described in Chapter 4 are suitable and there is also a guidance document entitled *Assessing Pupils' Eligibility for Additional Time* available on the QCDA website. This lists assessment resources that are recognised as fit for purpose (but not necessarily recommended) for use in this context.

Be aware that this is an online procedure, with a strict deadline each year.

# Access arrangements during general and vocational examinations in secondary schools

As SENCO in a secondary school, you are responsible for setting up and managing a robust system throughout the school for identifying pupils who have difficulties accessing the curriculum and coping with their work due to literacy and/or other difficulties. With National Tests data, other information coming through from feeder schools, screening carried out in Year 7, school test results, subject teachers' reports and so on, most pupils with special educational needs will have been identified long before the beginning of the GCSE courses in Year 10.

However, there may be pupils who slip through the net for one reason or another. Sometimes the difficulties of hardworking and fairly bright children do not really become apparent until the increased demands on their reading and writing skills place them under noticeable stress. But on the whole, you should know the names of students who may require access arrangements during their GCSE courses and examinations by Year 9.

For England, Wales and Northern Ireland (for Scotland, see page 105), your primary reference is the *current* edition of **Access Arrangements, Reasonable Adjustments and Special Consideration**, published each year on behalf of all the Awarding Bodies by:

> Joint Council for Qualifications (JCQ)
> 29 Great Peter Street
> London SW1P 3LW
> www.jcq.org.uk

> **Make sure you are relying on the correct edition, sent to each school in September each year. This is also available online (click on 'JCQ top ten publications').**

There is no alternative to studying the regulations carefully each year and making sure that you completely understand them. The booklet always summarises, near the beginning, any changes from the previous year and contains illustrative case studies. Appendix 7 (JCQ 2010–11) comprises three pages of Frequently Asked Questions, with the answers.

You will also find much useful information about the rationale for access arrangements and the responsibilities of Heads of Centres (and governors), Exams Officers and SENCOs in Jones, A. (ed.), 2011, **Dyslexia: Assessing the need for Access Arrangements during Examinations. A Practical Guide**; fourth edition, published jointly by JCQ and Patoss and available from Patoss.

Patoss publishes a new edition of the Practical Guide every few years to reflect any changes to the regulations and to describe new tests that have come onto the market, so the content of this modestly priced publication remains substantially accurate and valid over the years. Within its pages there are:

- Separate notes for head teachers, exams officers, subject teachers, learning support staff and SENCOs

- Photocopiable **Guidelines** for school staff as well as for candidates with dyslexia or other learning difficulties about access arrangements during public examinations.

You could photocopy these documents, or compose your own, to use in an 'awareness campaign' directed at colleagues, students and their parents during Year 9. *Everybody* concerned needs to know what the rules are.

In this context, two points are worth making as often as possible!

**Firstly,** access arrangements are designed to make 'reasonable adjustments' to the examination conditions, for those candidates who really need them – not to give unfair advantage to anyone. Access arrangements should enable a candidate with, for example, literacy difficulties (whatever the reason), or a sensory impairment, to cope with the examination for which he has been appropriately entered, given his level of knowledge and skill.

A misconception still held by some parents and teachers is that a diagnosis of dyslexia is in itself sufficient reason for their son or daughter to be granted extra time during an examination. This is a thorny topic and has led to much dispute in the past.

So, to be clear: the primary evidence required by the Awarding Bodies is that there is valid **evidence of need** – that is, on a **relevant** standardised test (e.g. of reading, spelling or cognitive processing) the student has a standardised score in the **below average** range (i.e. less than 85 – see page 9) and so needs substantially more time or assistance (e.g. a reader) than the majority of his peers, to show what he knows and can do.

This straightforward requirement set out by the JCQ is deemed a fair, transparent and practical means for the examination boards to provide for candidates with special educational needs, given the very large numbers they deal with each year.

**Secondly,** *last-minute* assessments and applications are generally inappropriate and should very rarely be necessary. The examinations come at the end of a long process of assessment, monitoring and (in some cases) learning support. This is because – for Key Stage 2 National Tests, GCSE and A level – an important part of the evidence required to support the granting of access arrangements is that they reflect the candidate's **normal way of working** and the **help he normally receives in the classroom.**

As SENCO, it is your responsibility (together with your head teacher and the governors) to manage all of this, although – unless you are a teacher who has undertaken specialist training – you will *not* be qualified to carry out the **formal diagnostic assessment** required by the Awarding Bodies (OCR, AQA, Edexcel, etc.), which is the other piece of the evidence requirement for each candidate.

## Who can do these reports?

Up until 1997, educational psychologists were the only professionals who could report on a pupil's need for special arrangements. This meant that a great many students were unable to apply, because they had no access to an educational psychologist – a clearly unacceptable situation. So the decision was then taken to accept reports from specialist teachers who had completed the original RSA Diploma for teaching students with Specific Learning Difficulties (SpLDs), since *assessment* was part and parcel of the course. Graduates of other postgraduate courses, which incorporated the theory and practice of educational testing in their training, were soon also 'approved' by the Joint Council.

**screening** exercise will, in addition, help identify those pupils who should be assessed and will prove cost effective.

# Screening

A timed test, which can be administered to groups or whole classes during an English lesson, is an extremely practical method of identifying most of the pupils whose difficulties are severe enough to warrant special arrangements.

## Writing speed

This is a tricky topic because pupils write slowly for a variety of reasons and the skills of a specialist teacher or educational psychologist may be needed to tease out the precise cause. However, the assessment method developed by Penny Allcock (2001) costs nothing and will certainly give you a reasonable indication of which students may need to be seen by a Specialist. The background to this assessment and photocopiable downloads are on the Patoss website: www. patoss-dyslexia.org

Most teachers who use this method get the students to count the words in their own free-writing sample and then double-check a paragraph or two in those whose scores are low, to verify the results. Your own quick visual inspection will reveal those scripts where the handwriting and/or spelling is so poor that legibility is a real issue, although subject teachers should already have flagged up this particular problem.

*Note:* This assessment method is currently accepted by the JCQ for updating reports on pupils in the first two groups, since it enables you to state whether these candidates' free writing speed (in words per minute) is in the below-average range for their age.

## Reading tests

Arguably, it is not the most productive use of your resources to **screen** for reading difficulties, since the group identified as having difficulties via the writing test (see above) will almost certainly include all your poor readers. Furthermore, quick single-word tests will not pick out pupils who have trouble with comprehension.

If you administer a longer, more comprehensive reading test, the specialist teacher or educational psychologist cannot use the results, since she is not permitted to include data in assessment reports unless she has personally administered the test. Remember also, that the *same* test cannot be used again, due to possible 'practice effects'.

However, if you do wish to screen for reading ability, the following resources would be suitable since they are age-appropriate, reasonably up to date, give standardised scores and have parallel forms enabling retesting by a specialist:

- **Access Reading Test**, published by Hodder Education
  *Age range:* 7–20 years; *Time needed:* 30 minutes

- **Hodder Group Reading Test 3**, 2nd edition, published by Hodder Education
  *Age range:* 9:5 – 16+ years; *Time needed:* 30 minutes
- **New Group Reading Test**, published by GL Assessment
  *Age range:* 6–16 years; *Time needed:* about 45–50 minutes
- **Suffolk Reading Scale**, published by GL Assessment
  *Age range:* 6–17:4; *Time needed:* 30 minutes

**To conclude:** having identified all the pupils who definitely or may need access arrangements, by Easter of Year 9, select those for whom either an updated or first assessment report is required. Refer these pupils to the specialist teacher or educational psychologist who is nominated by your head teacher to carry out the assessments.

Make sure you have all the relevant information relating to **evidence of need** and **history of provision** on file and easily accessible, so that the applications online can be completed where necessary or in case of inspection by the JCQ. See chapter 5 of the current regulations (2010–11) regarding this stage of the process – especially paragraph 5.7, which lists the arrangements which must be applied for online and those that may not.

Time for proper liaison with the specialist teacher needs to be allocated so that you can jointly discuss each pupil's needs and appropriate access arrangements once all the evidence and information is to hand. Make sure all the information is passed on to the examinations officer **in good time** so that applications for access arrangements and modified papers can be submitted by the stated deadlines each year.

From now on, your main task, together with colleagues (learning support staff, examinations officer), is to ensure that all necessary resources and arrangements are put in place. Each pupil, and his parents, must also be informed about what has been agreed.

Finally, some training in using the particular arrangement sensibly should be provided, so that the student can practise during mock exams and then reap the benefit during the actual GCSE.

## Key differences regarding access arrangements during KS2 National Tests compared to public examinations

In the **secondary** school, extra time is usually at the discretion of the SENCO, but she must apply to the examination boards for permission to provide readers, scribes and so on. In the **primary** school setting, the reverse is true – it is extra time that must be applied for during Key Stage 2 tests, but all other access arrangements are notified by the SENCO to the local authority.

Teachers often ask why there is a major procedural difference between the regulations for National Tests and GCSE/A level. The answer is that they have been developed by different organisations for somewhat different purposes. The aim of National Tests is to gauge how well a school is developing its pupils' attainments in the core curriculum subjects. Public examinations, on the other hand, measure each individual candidate's knowledge and skills in a wide variety of subjects and the student will go on to *use* his qualifications in applications for further education, training and employment.

# Access arrangements in Scotland

In Scotland, you need the ***Introduction to Assessment Arrangements for Schools and Colleges*** published by:

> Scottish Qualifications Authority
> The Optima Building,
> 58 Robertson Street
> Glasgow
> G2 8DQ
>
> www.sqa.org.uk (click on the *Equalities* section to find all the access arrangements documents)

The broad principles have much in common with those described above:

- Requests for special *assessment arrangements* should only be made on behalf of candidates who will be placed at a *substantial disadvantage* during the examinations.

- Candidates should have the ability to achieve national standards but be unable to do so using published assessment arrangements: the skills and competencies required for awards must still be met.

- Adjustments to the assessment arrangements should be tailored to meet the candidate's individual needs and should reflect his normal way of working.

The Scottish authorities place considerable emphasis on the need for early identification of special educational needs and provision of appropriate learning support so that a **portfolio of evidence** is gradually compiled during the secondary phase for each pupil. By the time the examination units/courses start, each candidate's needs should be well known and discussions can ensue with the student, teaching and learning support staff as to what arrangements might be suitable for him. The Head of Centre must then submit a request with appropriate evidence. This would normally consist of the existing working file containing notes of meetings, earlier assessments and Learning Support records, together with evidence that the candidate himself has been involved in the discussions about exam arrangements. For some particular access arrangements (e.g. use of a scribe), specific assessment data must be collated in support of the application.

# Music exams and access arrangements

For primary and secondary school pupils taking graded examinations in singing or playing an instrument, access arrangements such as extra time for sight-reading tasks are available for candidates with learning difficulties or disabilities. The evidence required in support of an application is currently:

- an assessment report from an educational psychologist or specialist teacher;
- a letter from the SENCO or head teacher at the pupil's school, or from the local authority.

The report or letter is valid for three years.

Detailed information is available from The Associated Board of the Royal Schools of Music, via their website: www.abrsm.org

Contact:

> Access Coordinator
> The Associated Board of the Royal Schools of Music
> 24 Portland Place
> London W1B 1LU
> *telephone:* 020 7467 8247
> *e-mail:* accesscoordinator@abrsm.ac.uk

---

## In conclusion ...

There is increasing parity between the regulations concerning access arrangements across the different phases of education, regardless of the awarding bodies concerned. All are complying with the principles enshrined in the *Disability Discrimination Act* (superseded by the Equality Act in 2010). Despite differences in the detail and required procedures – the reason why it is so important to keep abreast of each examining authority's current regulations each year – the *'reasonable adjustments duty'* underpins them all and states that *'You are required to take reasonable steps to avoid substantial disadvantage where a provision, criterion or practice puts disabled pupils at a substantial disadvantage'*.

*(Equality and Human Rights Commission,* www.equalityhumanrights.com *)*

# Glossary

| | |
|---|---|
| **ADD** | Attention Deficit Disorder |
| **ADHD** | Attention Deficit Hyperactivity Disorder |
| **AfL** | Assessment for Learning |
| **APP** | Assessing Pupils' Progress |
| **ASD** | Autistic Spectrum Disorders |
| **BDA** | British Dyslexia Association |
| **BPS** | British Psychological Society |
| **CA** | Chronological Age |
| **CoP** | Code of Practice |
| **CT** | Class Teacher |
| **DCD** | Developmental Coordination Disorder (dyspraxia) |
| **EAL** | English as an Additional Language |
| **ECaR** | Every Child a Reader |
| **EP** | Educational Psychologist |
| **EYFS** | Early Years Foundation Stage |
| **HFW** | High Frequency Word |
| **IEP** | Individual Education Plan |
| **IQ** | Intelligence Quotient |
| **JCQ** | Joint Council for Qualifications |
| **KS** | Key Stage |
| **LD** | Learning Difficulty |
| **LS** | Learning Support |
| **LSCWC** | Look Say Cover Write and Check |
| **NC** | National Curriculum |
| **NLS** | National Literacy Strategy |
| **OT** | Occupational Therapist |
| **PATOSS** | Professional Association of Teachers of Students with Specific Learning Difficulties |
| **RA** | Reading Age |
| **SEN** | Special Educational Needs |
| **SENSS** | Special Educational Needs Support Service |
| **SENCO** | Special Educational Needs Coordinator |
| **SLCN** | Speech, Language and Communication Needs |
| **SLT** | Speech and Language Therapist |

| | |
|---|---|
| **SMART** | Specific, Measurable, Attainable/Achievable, Relevant, Time-limited |
| **SMARTER** | as SMART, *plus* Evaluated and Reviewed |
| **SPAG** | Spelling, Punctuation and Grammar |
| **SpLD** | Specific Learning Difficulties |
| **SA** | Spelling Age |
| **SD** | Standard Deviation |
| **SS** | Standardised Score |
| **TA** | Teaching Assistant |

# References

Allcock, P. (2001) *Assessment of Handwriting Speed*, PATOSS website www.patoss-dyslexia.org

Backhouse, G. & Morris, K. (2005). *Dyslexia? Assessing and reporting. The Patoss Guide.* Hodder Education.

Baldwin, L (2006) *I Hear with my Little Ear,* Cambridge; LDA.

Brand, V. (1984) *Spelling Made Easy*, Wakefield; Egon.

Burton, S. (2004) Self-esteem groups for secondary pupils with dyslexia. *Educational Psychology in Practice*, 20, (1), pp 55–73.

Clay, M. (1972) *The Early Detection of Reading Difficulties.* Auckland: Heinemann.

Fredrickson et al (1997) *Phonological Assessment Battery* (PhAB), GL Assessment.

Hatcher, P. J. (2000), *Sound Linkage,* Pearson.

Hawker, G. T. (1981) *Spell it Yourself*, Oxford University Press.

Hickey, K. (1977) *Hickey Multisensory Language Course*, Whurr.

Hoover, W. A. & Gough, P. B. (1990) The simple view of reading. *Reading and Writing: an Interdisciplinary Journal. 2*, 127–60.

JCQ (2010/11) *Access Arrangements, Reasonable Adjustments and Special Consideration*, www.jcq.org.uk

Jones, A. (ed.) (2011) *Dyslexia: Assessing the need for Access Arrangements during Examinations*, Evesham; Patoss.

*Letters and Sounds* (2007) www.standards.dfes.gov.uk

*Literacy for all. Support for children and young people with literacy difficulties/dyslexia* (2009). London Borough of Newham Learning Support Service. Contact: maggie.noon@newham.gov.uk

Lohman, D, Hagen, E. & Thorndike, R. (2001) *Cognitive Abilities Test*, Third edition (CAT3), GL Assessment.

Miskin, R. (2000) *Read Write Inc,* Oxford University Press.

Muter, V., Hulme, C. & Snowling, M. (1997) *Phonological Abilities Test* (PAT), Pearson.

*Primary National Strategy* (2009) Department for Education and Skills www.teachernet.gov.uk/publications

QCDA, Key Stage 2 Assessment and Reporting Arrangements (ARA).

Raven, J. et al (2008) *Ravens Standard Progressive Matrices & Mill Hill Vocabulary Scale*, Pearson.

Rose, J. (2006) *Independent review of the teaching of early reading: final report,* www.standards.dfes.gov.uk/phonics/rosereview

Rose, J. (2009) *Identifying and Teaching Children and Young People with Dyslexia and Literacy Difficulties.* Department for Children, Schools and Families. www.teachernet.gov.uk/publications

Speake, J. (2003) *How to Identify and Support Children with Speech and Language Difficulties.* Cambridge; LDA.

Torgeson, J, K. (2007) Recent discoveries from research on remedial interventions for children with dyslexia. In M. J. Snowling and C. Hulme (Eds), *The Science of Reading: A Handbook.* Oxford: Blackwell (pp 521–37).

Topping, K. (1995) *Paired Reading, Writing & Spelling.* London; Cassell.

# Useful Organisations

**Major UK test publishers**

GL Assessment www.gl-assessment.co.uk

Hodder Education www.hoddertests.co.uk

Pearson Assessment www.psychcorp.co.uk

Afasic – Association for all Speech Impaired Children www.afasicengland.org.uk

ASLTIP – Association of Speech & Language Therapists in Independent Practice www.helpwithtalking.com

Autism Education Trust www.theautismeducationtrust.org.uk

British Association of Occupational Therapists & College of Occupational Therapists www.cot.co.uk

British Dyslexia Association www.bdadyslexia.org.uk

British Psychological Society www.bps.org.uk

Communications Trust www.thecommunicationstrust.org.uk

Chartered Society of Physiotherapists www.csp.org.uk

Dyslexia Action www.dyslexiaaction.org.uk

Dyslexia-SpLD Trust www.thedyslexia-spldtrust.org.uk

Dyspraxia Foundation www.dyspraxiafoundation.org.uk

Helen Arkell Dyslexia Centre (for training and resources) www.arkellcentre.org.uk

Iansyst Ltd (for assistive technology) www.iansyst.com

I CAN (for children with communication difficulties) www.ican.org.uk

Joint Council for Qualifications www.jcq.org.uk

National Handwriting Association www.nha-handwriting.org.uk

Partners in Education (for training and resources) www.partnersineducation.co.uk

PATOSS www.patoss-dyslexia.org

Royal College of Speech and Language Therapists www.rcslt.org

Smart Kids (UK) www.smartkids2.co.uk

The authors of this book hope it has whetted your appetite to further develop your skills in helping pupils with literacy difficulties. To find out more about training opportunities, you can contact Patoss, Dyslexia Action and/or the British Dyslexia Association via the websites above.